$$\frac{250}{y^2 \eta}$$

THE JEHOVAH'S WITNESSES

THE

Jehovah's Witnesses

By HERBERT HEWITT STROUP

NEW YORK · COLUMBIA UNIVERSITY PRESS · 1945

THE AMERICAN COUNCIL OF LEARNED SOCIETIES HAS GENEROUSLY
CONTRIBUTED FUNDS TO ASSIST IN THE PUBLICATION OF THIS VOLUME

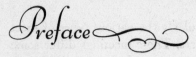

Preface

To INVESTIGATE a widespread, socially meaningful organization like the Jehovah's Witnesses is a herculean task for any one researcher, yet such has been my effort. During a period of several years I have sought, through various means, to acquaint myself scientifically with the Jehovah's Witnesses. This purpose has not been an easy one, although probably I would not have enjoyed it half so much had it been so.

The Witnesses awaken tremendously complex reactions. To the person interested in current affairs they present a vital problem, because of their attitude toward the nation, its flag and symbols, its stake in the second World War, and the deeper and underlying problems concerning the significance of democracy and freedom. For the person interested in the nature of religion and its many varying ramifications the Witnesses contribute much significant data. While opposed to all traditional religious associations, they have developed their own particular interpretation of the character of personal and social religion. More specifically, the failure of the Christian churches to create a highly satisfactory medium of expression for the needs and aspirations of the underprivileged can in part be seen in this movement. For the person who, with abstraction, seeks to understand the character of human motivation in general and the sociological nature of the "sect," the Jehovah's Witnesses furnishes present and powerful resources.

The main basis of the work which I have done is observation. In the course of preparing this interpretation I have sought to secure my information chiefly through the medium of participation in the activities, both public and private, of the Witnesses themselves. For some time after beginning the study I did not even make a systematic survey of the official literature, because I wished, above all else, to understand the Witnesses for themselves and without the bias which might come from a somewhat artificial approach to their organization. Only late in my investigation did I deem it necessary and proper to create a historical and literary frame for my findings. That such a frame is highly important in terms of the final estimate of the group I do not doubt in the least, and one can find in this account the results of my belief. But, first and foremost, I have sought to understand the Witnesses as people.

One of the methods employed in seeking to understand the Witnesses themselves was to make as many personal contacts as possible with their

way of life. To that end I attended regularly the various types of meetings which the Jehovah's Witnesses offers. These meetings differ somewhat from section to section of the country, and occasionally I have
mentioned in the body of my report the meaning of these sectional variations. Furthermore, to secure my information I spent considerable time
in friendly association with some of the Witnesses. This involved "canvassing" with them on the streets of certain cities, entering their homes
for social occasions, eating at their tables, even visiting them in jail. In
order that these personal contacts might have a more objective bearing,
I undertook several hundred case studies and made detailed reports
for my own use on all aspects of the movement that seemed of chief
importance.

Unfortunately, in many respects, I could not obtain that kind of information from the Witnesses themselves or from their leaders from
which a more statistical report could have been prepared. To the casually
interested person, this failure may signify the lack of hard work on my
part, but this, I make bold to claim, is too hasty a judgment. In planning the investigation, I sought to create several questionnaires for use
in securing quite definite information. I found, all too quickly, that the
questionnaires led to a lessening of rapport between myself and member
Witnesses. Since the movement is in many ways a "secret" one, the members were loathe to give me openly any information. Moreover, the leaders issued orders to all local groups that I should not be aided in any direct way in securing my information. Even as late as November, 1943,
the present leader of the Witnesses, Mr. N. H. Knorr, informed me by
letter that the "Society does not have the time, nor will it take the time,
to assist you in your publication concerning Jehovah's witnesses." Indeed,
according to the incumbent President of the Society, aside from the scant
materials to be found in the brief *Yearbook*, "there is no other information that we have available to the public."

My information has, therefore, come the hard way. For the most part
what I have uncovered, while on the surface it may look inadequate,
is about all that is known concerning the organization at the present.
Probably a detailed study of the movement is available to a very few of
the Witness leaders only. In many ways, mine is a pioneering venture.
There is no detailed and accurate study with which I could check my findings. In regard to the experiences of the Witnesses themselves I have
sought wherever possible and practical to select from the official literature

those personal testimonies which would provide a later researcher with a fairly sure means of checking the present findings. I do not assume to have exhausted the possibilities of research upon the Jehovah's Witnesses. Indeed, I am well aware of certain limitations which my study involves, both as to approach and to findings.

For assistance in the preparation of this study, I am indebted to many more persons and organizations than can be mentioned here. From Professor Horace M. Kallen of the Graduate Faculty of Political and Social Science of the New School for Social Research, I received valued aid in the construction of the whole project. He has given me much from his storehouse of wisdom and experience. Professor Carl Mayer of the same institution also contributed intelligent guidance. The American Civil Liberties Union opened its files and services to me. The American Council of Learned Societies, through the awarding of a grant, made possible in large part the publication of the findings. My thanks are extended to various members of the Columbia University Press staff for their generous aid, and especially to Miss Matilda Berg for her detailed assistance. Mrs. Anna E. D. Guldin of Reading, Pennsylvania, and Mr. and Mrs. William V. Stroup of Philadelphia, Pennsylvania, were also helpful in many ways. To the Witnesses themselves I owe a tremendous debt both for the personal and for the formal instruction which they tendered me. Finally, my largest obligation is extended to my wife, Grace, who, with patience, hard work, and skill has undergirded the entire undertaking. She is a living testimony to the fact that a woman can be both Martha and Mary. Needless to say, responsibility for the final form of the study rests upon me.

HERBERT H. STROUP

Brooklyn College
January, 1945

Contents

History and Leaders

INTO THE FOREGROUND of the American scene has come in recent years a movement which is one of the most striking and interesting examples of truly American religious creativity. This movement is popularly known as the Jehovah's Witnesses. Although the organization had its origin over seventy years ago, and largely gained its present strength some twenty-five years ago, it has been only recently that its refusal to salute any flag or to enter any army, and its willingness to submit to persecution have brought it into international surveillance. But aside from its present prominence the movement clearly indicates certain general characteristics which make it worthy of detailed study as a typical American contribution to religious living.

Generally speaking, there are four predominant religious expressions which are typically American in their origin and development. The Mormons, now known as the Church of the Latter Day Saints, constitute the first. Founded in 1830 by Joseph Smith, Jr., at Fayette, New York, the group moved to Ohio, then to Missouri, and finally to Illinois, where Smith met death at the hands of a mob. Brigham Young, who succeeded Smith as the leader of the group, left Illinois in the spring of 1847 with 143 companions and arrived in July of that same year in the valley of the Great Salt Lake. Here the Mormons were confronted by many serious problems, but, dominated by the thought that their new settlement was their "promised land," and believing that God was the inspiration of their venture, they managed in the course of years to construct a community which is religious at its base. The Latter Day Saints are the first large-scale religious movement in this country which can be said to be original.

Christian Science, the religion founded by Mrs. Mary Baker Eddy in 1866, is another original American religious expression. Using the idea of "mind" over "matter" as the basis for the new religion, and believing all her teachings to be confirmed by the Bible, Mrs. Eddy quickly developed a system of belief which declared all evil to be illusory when properly understood and only the good to be real. The Mother Church, or the central church, was established in Boston in 1879 and today regulates some 3,000 branches of the organization all over the world. Arising in a period when Christianity (as expressed by the churches) and science were at loggerheads over their individual and collective significance as means of interpreting experience, this movement, happily for many, combined a sort of Christianity with a sort of science.

The third distinctly American religion is that of the Negro. The American Negro religion cannot precisely be classed with Mormonism and Christian Science because the Negroes are not an organized religious group in the same sense as the others, yet they have provided a part of the distinctively American religious culture. Developed through decades of social disability and intense suffering, the Negro religion has been productive of some of the finest expressions of truly American faith. These people, more than any other American group, have been able to personalize religious feeling, as their spirituals make evident:

> Nobody knows the trouble I'se seen,
> Nobody knows but Jesus.

Jehovah's Witnesses, launched at about the same time as Christian Science, is the fourth and one of the most complete examples in form and spirit of truly American religious society. The Jehovah's Witnesses has been classed with "social justice," a Roman Catholic movement founded by Father Charles E. Coughlin, of the Shrine of the Little Flower in Detroit, Michigan. The two cannot, however, be satisfactorily compared, for as Stanley High says: "Coughlin is a voice. Rutherford [the late leader of the Jehovah's Witnesses] is both a voice and a movement." [1] That is to say that whereas Coughlin organized the Union for Social Justice to bring about banking and labor reforms, he did so under the principles laid down for socially minded Roman Catholics by the *Rerum Novarum* of Pope Leo XIII. He did not present himself as the prophet of a new faith. The Jehovah's Witnesses, on the other hand, has developed a completely new religious system. Although it has roots which may be traced to other religious systems, nevertheless, it is ostensibly original and claims to have not only a new truth, but "the truth" which thus far in history has not been otherwise disclosed. [2] Separateness from all other religious organizations is one of the movement's cardinal tenets.

Although the religious movement now known as the Jehovah's Witnesses has always been a single organization, it has, during its history, been known by many other names. In 1872 when the group was first

---

[1] "Armageddon, Inc.," *Saturday Evening Post*, Sept. 14, 1940.
[2] *Jehovah's Servants Defended*, pp. 30–31.

organized there was some doubt among the followers of the founder, Mr. Charles Taze Russell, as to what they should properly be called. Mr. Russell promptly and emphatically announced: "We call ourselves simply CHRISTIANS." [3] But the desire to be so designated was not realized; in later years Dawnites, Russellites, Watch Tower Bible people, Bible Students, Rutherfordites, and many other names arose to confuse both those within and without the group. Just when the body came to be known as "Jehovah's Witnesses" was obscured further by the manner in which Mr. Russell's successor, Mr. Joseph Franklin Rutherford, answered inquiries about the origin of the name. In 1940 Mr. Malcolm Logan of the New York *Evening Post* wrote to Mr. Rutherford asking twenty-three specific questions about the Jehovah's Witnesses, one of which was: "When did you adopt the name 'Jehovah's Witnesses,' and what were you called before then?" To this direct question Mr. Rutherford replied: "Jehovah's witnesses have been on earth as an organization for more than 5,000 years. (See Isaiah 43: 10–12; Hebrews 11th Chapter; John 18: 37.) All true Christians are Jehovah's Witnesses." [4] Mr. Rutherford, however, in *The Theocracy*,[5] admitted that the name "Jehovah's Witnesses" was unknown in the days of Mr. Russell's leadership.

If one studies the publications and the history of the movement one discovers that "Jehovah's Witnesses" was declared to be the official designation of the group by Mr. Rutherford himself in a resolution to that effect offered by him and passed by an international convention of Witnesses meeting at Columbus, Ohio, in 1931. In this resolution Mr. Rutherford described the confusion which resulted from the group's lack of an official name. He said that the organization could not assume "the name of any man" as its official title, but he resolved that his followers should be identified as "Jehovah's Witnesses." [6] In another publication, Mr. Rutherford explained the use of the term at greater length:

Today there is but one class of men and women under the sun who have faith and courage to deliver the message of truth concerning the fall of "Christendom" and of Satan's entire organization and concerning the hope for the people in the kingdom of God, and that class or company of people is made up of those who are fully devoted to Jehovah and to his kingdom. . . . While they love Charles T. Russell for his work's sake, as a follower of Christ,

[3] *Watch Tower*, Feb., 1884.   [4] *Judge Rutherford Uncovers the Fifth Column*, p. 20.
[5] Pp. 32 ff.   [6] *Ibid.*, pp. 36–38.

they cannot properly be called "Russellites." While they are students of the Bible, they cannot rightly be called by the name "Bible Students" or "Associated Bible Students." They are the followers of no man. Having been bought with the blood of Christ Jesus, justified and begotten by Jehovah, and called to his kingdom, and being wholly and unreservedly devoted thereto, they delight to take the name the Lord gave them, which is JEHOVAH'S WITNESSES.[7]

Since 1931, therefore, the group has been known as the "Jehovah's Witnesses," although this name has not succeeded completely in eliminating some of the others by which the group has in the past been distinguished.[8]

The Jehovah's Witnesses was founded in 1872 by Charles Taze Russell in Allegheny (now a suburb of Pittsburgh) Pennsylvania. There is no unified historical record of the movement and on the whole the present-day followers are totally ignorant that the group has a history. The majority of those whom I questioned did not even know the year of its founding. Many Witnesses would like to assume that the organization, being inspired of God, never had an earthly beginning. Some actually told me that it dated back to a period before the creation of the world. Others said that the problem of the organization's history was trivial beside such a monumental task as that in which they were now engaged.

The official publications of the movement demonstrate a similar unconcern. The *Yearbook* states simply that in 1872 "a few Christian persons met together in a little house in Pennsylvania to consider the Scriptures relative to the coming of Christ and His Kingdom." Nothing is recorded of these "few Christian persons" until 1884 when they were sufficiently numerous to organize themselves as a corporation which they termed "The Zion's Watch Tower Society." The official publications mention that the corporation title was changed, in 1909, when the headquarters were moved to Brooklyn, New York, to that of "The People's Pulpit Association." Other publications state that in 1914, when the movement spread to England, a new corporation was formed under the laws of that country and called "The International Bible Students Association." Today the group in the United States is incorporated in New York and Pennsylvania as "The Watch Tower Bible and Tract Society." This meager information is all that the Society officially discloses.

From extensive and rigorous research, however, a fuller history can

[7] *The Kingdom*, p. 22.

[8] Although Mr. Rutherford never capitalized the word "Witnesses," in this study it is always capitalized when designating either the individual members or the group itself. This rule does not hold, however, in the case of quotations.

be pieced together. It properly begins with the life story of the founder, Charles Taze Russell. He was born the second son of Joseph L. and Ann Eliza (Birney) Russell, at Pittsburgh, Pennsylvania, in 1852. Nothing can be discovered about his elder brother and it is not known whether he had any sisters, as none ever received mention in his writings. Russell was extremely fond of his father and seems to have been more deeply affected by him than by his mother, who died when he was nine years old. The father, who was one of the first converts to the religious movement started by his son, presented $1,000 to the young leader that he might spread the new message. This amount of money, Russell said, was "a large donation for his means." In his later years the father retired to Florida where he sought to win others to the movement. He wrote frequently to his son and these letters were often published in the Society's magazine, evidently to show the followers the fine relationship which existed between the son and the father. The elder Russell wrote repeatedly that he was proud of his son and believed that Jehovah was leading him for a great purpose.[9]

Little is known of Charles Russell's early years. Mr. Meta Sturgeon, his private secretary, claimed that Russell was unable to attend college because of his responsibilities to his father's business, which necessitated his traveling between certain cities in the Pittsburgh area. He and his father owned and managed a chain of five clothing stores. Young Russell did, according to this source, have the benefit of private tutors.[10]

In 1906 Russell wrote of the experience he had in founding the new movement:

Let me begin the narrative at the year 1868 when the Editor [Russell] having been a consecrated child of God for some years, and a member of the Congregational church and of the Young Men's Christian Association, began to be shaken in faith regarding many long-accepted doctrines. Brought up a Presbyterian and indoctrinated from the catechism and being naturally of an inquiring mind, I fell an easy prey to the logic of infidelity as soon as I began to think for myself. But that which at first threatened to be the utter shipwreck of faith in God and the Bible was, under God's providence overruled for good, and merely wrecked my confidence in human creeds and systems of misrepresentation of the Bible.

Gradually I was led to see that though each of the creeds contained some elements of truth, they were on the whole misleading and contradictory of

[9] *Watch Tower*, May, 1888.   [10] *Ibid.*, Feb., 1916.

God's word. Among other theories I stumbled upon Adventism. Seemingly by accident one evening I dropped into a dusty, dingy hall where I heard religious services were held, to see if the handful who met there had anything more sensible to offer than the creeds of the great churches. There for the first time I heard something of the views of Second Adventism, the preacher being Mr. Jonas Wendell, long since deceased. Thus I confess indebtedness to Adventists as well as to other denominations. Though his Scripture expositions were not entirely clear, and though it was very far from what we now rejoice in, it was sufficient under God to re-establish my wavering faith in the divine inspiration and to show that the records of the apostles and prophets are indissolubly linked.[11]

There is a tradition common among Witnesses who have been with the group for a number of years to the effect that Mr. Russell was a pious, orthodox Congregationalist until the time when, on one of his trips in caring for his father's business, he entered a poolroom to idle away a few moments. While in the poolroom someone engaged him in a conversation which led to biblical subjects and especially to the doctrine of hell. As a fundamentalist Christian, Russell sought vainly to defend the doctrine of hell against the verbal onslaughts of his opponent. Later, unable to forget the discussion, he set himself the task of examining the biblical foundation of the doctrine, and after a lengthy investigation concluded that it was unbiblical. This discovery led him to examine other popular Christian beliefs, many of which he also found faulty.

The group of Second Adventists to which Mr. Russell referred was founded by Mr. William Miller in 1829 and has also been called "Millerites." Miller's followers were largely composed of the economically dispossessed of the middle eastern states. Their principal belief was in the second coming of Jesus in the year 1840, and when this event did not take place, the believers lost faith and the group dissolved. Russell probably came into contact with some of those who clung to the faith even after the failure of their hope. He was certain the Second Adventists were "called of God" and that they were precursors of his movement. They comprised the one religious denomination that he did not completely condemn.[12]

Charles Russell was the chief motivating force in the religious group which he founded, and to him the small group of eager followers looked

[11] *Ibid.*, July, 1906. [12] Russell, *Studies in the Scriptures*, II, 240.

in all matters of belief and practice. His natural charm, his seeming broad-mindedness, his devotion to the Bible, his extreme claims, all won him devotees in the early years. Russell was always willing to meet people and to talk with them. On his lengthy speaking tours about the country he willingly posed for photographers, and thus left behind him a group of photographs which date the various stages of his life and career. He was a smallish man, thin and saintly in appearance. His demeanor, according to all available reports, was ascetic. In later life, his long white hair gave him the appearance of a modern patriarch. In speech, both public and private, his professionalized style marked him as a "spellbinder."

As larger audiences were reached, some of the followers ventured to suggest the formation of a new religious organization by which they might further spread the message. Accordingly, the Zion's Watch Tower Society was founded in 1884. Its work was divided among the faithful, whose ardor attracted others in great numbers. Thus motivated by the personality of the founder, the movement grew with remarkable speed.

To aid in the dissemination of his message, Russell set down his early views in a volume called *Food for Thinking Christians,* which he published about 1880, reportedly with some $40,000 of his own money. (The source of this personal contribution is not revealed.) In 1879 he established a magazine named *Zion's Watch Tower and Herald of Christ's Presence.* The most systematic exposition of his views can be found in his seven-volume series of *Studies in the Scriptures* (also called *Millennial Dawn*), the last volume of which was published posthumously. A book of Russell's sermons was also published after his death. Millions of copies of these works were distributed—a circulation of more than fifteen million was claimed for the seven-volume *Studies.* But, in accordance with Witness rule, Russell never collected royalties on his publications. Copies were sold for a nominal fee—twenty-five cents for a book and five cents for a pamphlet—and free copies were given to those who could not pay for them. Theoretically no one is supposed to make money on Witness publications, but I have seen no statistics to prove that this is the case.

The scope of the Society was broadened when, in 1880, Russell sent Mr. J. C. Sunderlin to England to open up a branch office for the distribution of literature in that country.[13] By 1888 "the word" was being

[13] *Watch Tower,* Oct., 1881.

preached throughout the United States and England and in such distant places as China, Africa, India, Turkey, and Haiti.[14] The missionary activities of the young movement were limited to the strict preaching of "the gospel." The missionaries did not attempt to introduce schools, hospitals or other institutions among those to whom they preached; the second coming of Jesus was too imminent for that.

At home the work of the Zion's Watch Tower Bible and Tract Society was carried on by a Board of Directors. Russell was president, and the rest of the Board consisted of W. I. Manor, vice president, M. F. Russell (not known to be a member of Russell's family), secretary and treasurer, and three others. Voting for the Board was open only to those who had contributed either at one time or over a period the sum of ten dollars to the Society. The contributor was entitled to one vote; for each additional contribution of ten dollars he was permitted another vote. The arrangement for the yearly elections, aside from that for the subsidiary offices, was always perfunctory, as Russell was the willingly acknowledged leader. When by 1909 the movement had grown large enough to warrant permanent international headquarters, the Society was moved to Brooklyn, New York, and was incorporated as the People's Pulpit Association. The same elective system of management was retained in the new corporation.

The Board, however, was merely a formal or legal organizational structure, for the real control and authority rested solely upon Russell. As the leader of the movement, he was a constant target for all sorts of criticism. Opposition, however, tended merely to strengthen his position with most of his followers. Naturally his new movement brought intensely bitter reactions from all of the established churches, liberal and conservative, Protestant and Roman Catholic. Even some of Russell's own followers came to consider him as "this boldly-conceited teacher," whose claim to divine inspiration surpassed that of the Bible writers; in 1909 twenty-nine believers seceded because of it.[15] Yet in the *Watch Tower* of July, 1906, Russell had written, "I claim nothing of superiority or supernatural power." He did, however, actually believe that he held a divinely appointed position. In one of his works he likened himself to a "Combination Timelock." The course of history now called

[14] *Ibid.*, Dec. 1888.

[15] J. H. Burridge, *Pastor Russell's Position and Credentials and His Methods of Interpretation*, p. 20.

for the "opening" of the divine secrets which comprised the theological treasure of his movement and he was the only one who knew the "combination."

Perhaps the most significant schismatic difficulty which Mr. Russell met in the leadership of his flock was that which arose from his divorce from Maria (Ackley) Russell, whom he had married in 1879. During the early years of their marriage, Mrs. Russell was a devoted follower of "the new truth." When the work of editing a widely circulated magazine became onerous to her husband, she frequently answered letters which were sent to him. Some of this correspondence appeared in the Society's magazine. When Mr. Russell was called upon to deliver lectures throughout this country and abroad, she also went on lecture tours, speaking to assemblies of women believers.

The couple had no children. In 1897 they were separated and in 1913 Mrs. Russell brought suit for divorce on four grounds: "That his conceit, egotism, and domination were such as to make life intolerable to any sensitive woman; that his conduct in relation to other women was improper; that on one occasion he was silent to his wife for four weeks and only communicated with her by letters of a reproachful character"; and "that he sought by most despicable means to isolate his wife from society, and designed to get her pronounced insane in order to put her away." In reviewing the case today, an observer may perceive that the evidence of the prosecution was not as conclusive as the jury considered it to be. One sample of the testimony indicates its circumstantiality. Mrs. Russell was being questioned on a point of central importance in the granting of the divorce.

Q. I want you to tell us what your husband did in company with this woman Rose, in your presence and in your home.

A. One evening I spent the evening downstairs, and our library and bedroom were next to each other upstairs on the second floor, and I spent the evening downstairs reading, and I went upstairs about ten o'clock to my room, and I supposed that he was either in the library or had retired, and when I went up there, I found he was in neither place, and I stepped out into the hall and there I found that he was in his night robe, sitting beside Miss Ball's bed and she was in bed. On other occasions I found him going in there, and I found that she called him in and said she wasn't well and wanted him in, and I objected to this, and I said that it was highly improper, and I said, "We have people about the house, and what kind of a name will be attached to this house, if you do that kind of thing?" and he got angry.

Q. You state that you found him doing this at other times. How often after that?

A. I found him a number of times; I don't remember how often.

Q. In her room?

A. Yes, sir. And I found him in the servant girl's room as well, and I found him locked in the servant girl's room.

Q. Did he make any explanation why he was in the girl's room?

A. No, he did not, he just got angry.[16]

Such a description of her husband's actions and relationships might have been true without proving that his behavior was in any sense immoral. Most of the testimony was highly suggestive but never conclusive. Additional evidence indicates that Mrs. Russell was generally suspicious of her husband's relations with other women and that at some point in their relationship she failed to understand completely the religiously inspired person's disregard for appearances.

Whatever the validity of the divorce case against Russell may have been, the results were nearly disastrous to his movement. Many of his followers felt that no one could be divinely directed (as they had believed their leader to be) and yet be divorced. Some openly charged Russell of grave immoralities and seriously questioned his veracity, and thousands of his disciples left the movement. After the case was closed, the Society offered in a current issue of the *Watch Tower* the sum of "$1,000 to be paid to the first party who proves in any court of justice in the United States that Pastor Russell is guilty of any immorality such as is the 'gossip' of those ministers who preach for pay." Sums of $50 and $10 also were offered for the production of various Bible texts which would prove that Russell's doctrines were false. The critics of Russell were answered by the head counsel (later the president) of the Society, Mr. J. F. Rutherford, in a pamphlet the title of which is suggestive of the extent to which the discontent had spread: *A Great Battle in the Ecclesiastical Heavens.*[17]

Mr. Russell publicly swore that he had never committed any such acts as those of which he was accused by his wife. He made public a "vow" in which he declared his intention never to enter any room in which one member of the opposite sex was alone, excepting a relative of the family. Until his death he required all of his followers to sign similar statements.

[16] J. J. Ross, *Some Facts and More Facts about the Self-Styled "Pastor" Russell*, pp. 25–31.

[17] Published in Brooklyn, N. Y., 1915.

He also prepared an affidavit, to be released upon his death, which denied any such immorality.

Despite the criticism against him, Mr. Russell was in great demand throughout the world for his lectures on the Bible and for his talks illustrated with stereopticon slides. His numerous trips throughout Europe and his tour around the world provided him with intimate knowledge of his worldwide organization. His duties were heavy, but he could not give up the fight he had begun. Embarked upon one of his country-wide lecture tours, he fell sick while on a private train and died on the Santa Fe route to Kansas on October 31, 1916. His last hours were described later by Sturgeon, his traveling companion and private secretary.

I called in the Pullman porter and the conductor and said, "We want you to see how a great man can die." The sight deeply impressed them, especially the porter. I called in the regular conductor and telegraphed for a physician to board the train at Panhandle [Texas], and he did. He saw the condition, recognized the correctness of the diagnosis and conclusion, gave me his name and was off before the train got under headway.

At one o'clock all were dismissed from the room, the door was locked, and we quietly watched over him until he breathed his last. We had observed the approaching signs of death before calling in the trainmen. . . . His quiet breathing became less frequent, his drooping eyelids opened like the petals of a flower and disclosed those eyes—those wonderful eyes, in all their magnificence—that we will never forget. Presently he breathed no more; we pressed our lips upon his noble brow, and knew that he had gone to be forever with and like the Lord, whom he loved so well.[18]

So died the creator of the movement known today as the Jehovah's Witnesses. He died, as must a founder of a religion which avows itself to take the place of all other religions, in the active promulgation of his beliefs.

Sincere as Russell was, his life was not unanimously evaluated as religiously and socially helpful. Some of the group left the movement, believing him to be the very incarnation of Satan. His embittered wife summoned up courage to say:

His life was one continuous round of expensive touring, at tremendous cost to many of his deceived followers. The "Watch Tower" of the 15th of March, 1911, page 92, to which my attention has been called, tells of a transcontinental tour of himself and company for 7,000 miles, beginning the 9th

[18] *Watch Tower*, Dec., 1916.

of June, the special train consisting of compartment, standard Pullman, and tourists' cars, the entire outfit stopping at the principle [*sic*] cities from New York to California, and holding meetings for about a month.

A similar tour was made before—I think, about a year previous. As I look at this pageantry, and consider what it all means, I am so thankful to my Lord who has delivered me from the snare, even though it was accomplished through fiery trial. . . .

At a convention he held about a year ago, near Lake Chautauqua, he and his special favorites were settled in palatial quarters apart from the main company. There he held daily receptions, to which five hundred each day were admitted by ticket, all being treated to refreshments, free boat ride, and carfare from the convention grounds to his quarters.[19]

To others, however, he was the divinely appointed means of salvation. To thousands of people the world over, Russell spoke the very words of God. They trusted him, they believed in him, and they were not disappointed. One man, forty years of age, wrote:

You do not know—O yes! I think that YOU do,—but certainly only a few can know what exceeding blessedness has come to me through my brief acquaintance with Mr. Russell and his works. How I wish there had been more.[20]

Some thought that their leader was close to Jehovah himself. The Preface of his posthumously published *Sermons* (it was written by Rutherford) says that he was used "by the Lord more than any other man on earth since the days of the apostles." Again, in the same work he was spoken of as the "most celebrated preacher of modern times," and of his voluminous writings it was noted:

His explanatory writings on the Bible are far more extensive than the combined writings of St. Paul, St. John, Arius, Waldo, Wycliffe, and Martin Luther—the Six Messengers to the church who preceded him.[21]

To these encomiums, Mr. Rutherford said:

St. Paul's greatness was due to the fact that the Lord used him most wonderfully to enlighten others concerning God's great Plan of Salvation for mankind. Since the days of the apostle Paul there have been other great reformers in the world. But, when the history of the Church of Christ is fully written, it will be found that the place next to St. Paul in the gallery of fame as an

19 J. H. Burridge, *Pastor Russell's Position*, p. 220.
20 *Watch Tower*, Sept. 1897.   21 *Sermons*.

expounder of the Gospel of the great Master will be occupied by CHARLES
TAZE RUSSELL.[22]

Upon the death of Russell the leadership of the group fell upon
the willing shoulders of Joseph Franklin Rutherford, who had been
chief legal counsel for the Society. Of the life of Mr. Rutherford little
accurate information is available. He is first mentioned in *Zion's Watch
Tower and Herald of Christ's Presence* in January, 1909, when he was
appointed by Mr. Russell as chairman of a business meeting for the election of officers to the Board. How long he had been connected with the
movement before that occasion cannot be ascertained accurately. Rutherford spoke only once of his introduction to "the truth." At the funeral
of Russell, he related the manner in which he came into the organization:

Long before I knew Pastor Russell he had done much for me. While I was
engaged in the law practice in the Middle West, there came into my office
one day a lady bearing some books in her arms. She was modest, gentle, and
kind. I thought she was poor, and that it was my privilege and duty to help
her. I found that she was rich in faith in God. I bought the books and afterwards read them. Up to that time I knew nothing about the Bible; I had
never heard of Pastor Russell. I did not even know that he was the author of
the books at the time I read them; but I know that the wonderfully sweet,
harmonious explanation of the plan of God thrilled my heart and changed the
course of my life from doubt to joy.[23]

Apparently from this record Mr. Rutherford was not in sympathy with
any church and did not believe in any sort of biblically founded religion
prior to his reading of the books of Charles Russell, a fact which seems
to be confirmed by other statements of his. The record indicates, moreover, that he came into "the truth" as did many other members, namely,
through the house-to-house "service work" of the Witnesses. Probably
he found his way into the inner sanctum because lawyers were greatly
needed by the organization and were seldom converted to it. At any
rate, by the time of Russell's death, Mr. Rutherford was an esteemed
member of the Board of Directors.

In January, 1917, the group held their annual business meeting in
Pittsburgh where elections for officers to the Board took place. Voting
at this meeting, as at all annual business meetings of the Witnesses, fell
upon those who had contributed ten dollars or more either in one sum
or over a period before the annual meeting. Some votes were cast by

[22] *Ibid.*, Preface.   [23] *Watch Tower*, Dec., 1916.

proxy. For members who could not attend, suitable forms were provided by the Society and were notarized before submission to the meeting. Some idea of the size of the Society and of financial contributions to it can be gained from the fact that approximately 150,000 votes were cast at the meeting which elected Mr. Rutherford. His name was the first to be suggested from the floor for the presidency. The nominations were closed and the entire vote was cast for him. There were two nominations for the vice presidency and only one for the office of secretary-treasurer.

After the elections, Mr. Rutherford "extemporaneously" addressed the thousands of assembled Witnesses:

Dear friends, I cannot let this occasion pass without saying a few words to you. My heart is full to overflowing. You will bear me witness that I have not in any way sought the office of President of this Society. Up to this hour I have not discussed it with anyone. I have purposely avoided doing so, believing that the Lord would accomplish his purpose. What has been done here today I feel that the Lord has directed, and I humbly submit to his will. To him alone is due all honor and glory.

It is a great privilege to be one of its [the Society's] officers. I am mindful of my inability to measure up to the full requirements.

One who follows a great man in office always finds it a more difficult task to fill the office than it was for his predecessor, due largely to the fact that his acts are measured by the high standard set and maintained by the great man who preceded him. Brother Russell was truly a great man, because especially fitted for the use to which the Lord put him. No one can fill his place. . . . I will continue to make known the glad tidings. . . . The policies which Brother Russell inaugurated I will attempt to carry forward. . . . There is much work for you and me to do. . . . In the performance of the duties of President I shall feel more keenly than ever that I am your servant. It is my desire to serve faithfully.[24]

Although Mr. Rutherford may have believed that the day's event was in accord with the will of God, many of the Witnesses did not. Following his election the existence of the movement was threatened as never before. Many of those who remembered wistfully the halcyon days of Mr. Russell's leadership found that the new incumbent did not fulfill their expectations of a saintly leader. Various elements split off from the parent body, and such fission continued throughout Rutherford's leadership. Among the groups which withdrew at various times are the Standfast Movement, the Paul Johnson Movement, the Elijah Voice Movement,

[24] *Ibid.*

the Eagle Society, and the Pastoral Bible Institute of Brooklyn. These seceding groups retained the essential theological message of Russell, but they could not give approval to the election of Mr. Rutherford as president of the Society.

Individually, and in the course of years, numerous Witnesses turned from the organization and the message of Rutherford. Usually this deflection occurred when he spoke too pointedly against some tenet close to the hearts of those who had been devoted followers of Russell. For example, a schism over the significance of the Great Pyramid of Egypt resulted in the withdrawal of many of the older participants in the movement. Russell had worked out an elaborate theory that the Great Pyramid clearly explained the whole history of the human race and that it was designed by Jehovah to foretell the time when Jesus would appear for the second time on earth. The coming of Jesus did not take place as planned by Russell, with the help of the pyramid, and the theory was promptly dropped. When Rutherford, as late as 1929, placed his official condemnation upon any attempt to find God's will outside of the Bible, using Russell's interpretation of the pyramid as an example, many left the movement. Rutherford especially warned these renegade Witnesses that they would certainly "suffer destruction" for their disobedience.[25]

Before his death, however, Rutherford had so skillfully organized the spread of his word and the working of the organization that no great number of malcontents reached the stage of a complete break from the movement. Occasionally the official magazines contain a letter from some Witness who had doubted the revelation of truth claimed by the Society but had battled his way back to faithful obedience.

Mr. Rutherford was generally called "Judge" by his followers and others, even as Mr. Russell was called "Pastor." Both these terms were complimentary. "Pastor" Russell never attended a theological seminary and had only the utmost scorn for those who did. Commonly he is said by Witnesses to have gained the right to be called "Pastor" by his zeal and service for the Lord. During his lifetime several thousands of small groups regularly elected him as their "Pastor." In a somewhat similar way, Mr. Rutherford became a "Judge." His right to the title of "Judge" came only by reason of his having served on several occasions in a lower court of a traveling circuit in Missouri. Mr. Rutherford, however, never referred to himself as "Judge." The conferring of these

[25] *The Kingdom*, p. 14.

titles seems evidence of an intense desire to elevate the leader in prestige and the organization to a status of openly authoritarian management and spirit.

To those who have seen him, Rutherford appeared, in Stanley High's words, "more like a senator than most senators." He stood and walked with a measured dignity not without impressiveness. He wore winged collars and bow ties, and held his glasses, which he used for reading and for effective gesturing, on a long black ribbon. His voice was an excellent one for public speaking, occasionally reaching a low-pitched fortissimo that deeply thrilled his audience.

Little is known of the private life of Mr. Rutherford. His name is not listed in *Who's Who in America*. His wife, Mary, unlike Mrs. Russell, took no active part in the Witness movement. She never made personal appearances at any of the Society's meetings, either alone or with her husband. There is only one reference to her in the official literature. This occurs in the Society's magazine for August, 1918, issued during Rutherford's imprisonment at Atlanta, Georgia. In a letter to the Society, Mr. Rutherford stated: "My dear wife arrived Friday and spent an hour with me." It was rumored among the Witnesses that the marital life of the Rutherfords was not serene. Some felt that an estrangement existed, but that the Rutherfords, having learned from the experience of Russell the effects of openly acknowledging such a condition, had come to an agreement that their marriage would to all appearances continue.

The Rutherfords had only one child, a son, Malcolm G. Rutherford. The Witnesses differed as to whether young Rutherford was in accord with his father's teachings; some declared him a full-time worker in the organization, while others pronounced him a renegade. In any event, the son took no prominent part in the movement.

Soon after assuming leadership of the Jehovah's Witnesses in 1917, Rutherford found himself confronted with the problem of the war into which the United States had entered. His predecessor had taught that war is unchristian, merely a sign of the end of the age and a preliminary worldly step before the righteous king, Jesus, would return to establish his celestial rule. Rutherford agreed with this interpretation and refused to support the war. As a consequence, he and seven associates were tried in a United States District Court in Brooklyn on four charges, two of which may be summarized as "a conspiracy to cause insubordination in the military and naval forces of the United States" and "a conspiracy to obstruct the recruiting and enlistment service of the United States." All the defendants were found guilty of violating the Espionage Act and were sentenced, with the exception of one Giovanni De Cecca, to serve twenty years in the Federal Penitentiary at Atlanta, Georgia, on each of the four counts; the four prison terms were to commence and run concurrently. De Cecca was sentenced to serve ten years in the same institution. The sentences of the eight began in June, 1918. In March of the following year, however, the defendants were admitted to bail, their cases having been appealed. In May of that year a higher court decided that a new trial should be granted. Since the war had ended and inasmuch as a new trial was expensive in time and money, the whole matter was dropped.

While in jail Rutherford continued to run the organization to which he had so lately fallen heir. A Witness tradition has it that he and his associates organized Bible study groups in the penitentiary and spread "the true word" among the other prisoners. By the end of his term, Rutherford is reported to have organized a Bible class of approximately two hundred members. From the penitentiary he wrote weekly letters to all the flock. These letters, obviously modeled after the prison epistles of Saint Paul, were published in the Society's magazine. A term in jail did not harm the prestige of Rutherford among his followers; the financial report shows an increase in contributions for the period.

Upon his release, Rutherford sought to follow out the principles of leadership so clearly developed by Russell. On several occasions Russell had engaged in debates with fundamentalist Christian ministers. Some of these debates were printed by his Society and millions of copies were distributed. Mr. Rutherford took part in similar debates; the report of the first in the Society's magazine described him as an able extemporaneous speaker. Once in 1933 he issued a proclamation to the Roman Catholic pope declaring his readiness to debate with the pope, or any representative officially designated by him, upon the causes of the persecution of the Witnesses.[26] He also challenged the Federal Council of the Churches of Christ in America to a radio debate upon the nature of religion and the causes of the Witness persecution. Rutherford suggested that each side pay half of the radio bill.[27] His offers received no attention.

In following out the pattern set by Russell, Rutherford wrote many

[26] Rutherford, *Religious Intolerance: Why?* p. 41.
[27] Rutherford *Jehovah's Witnesses: Why Persecuted?* p. 41.

books, pamphlets, and articles. The distribution figures of Russell's books —including about fifteen million copies of *Studies in the Scriptures*— are dwarfed by those of his successor. In 1940 Rutherford claimed that he had written ninety-nine books and pamphlets in the previous twenty years. His writings have appeared in seventy-eight languages, and over 300,000,000 items have been distributed.[28] After 1940 he published several more pamphlets and at least one more book.

Rutherford's writings are similar in many respects to Russell's. Both men bolstered what they wrote with innumerable scriptural quotations from every book of the Bible and nearly every verse. Both men employed a similar theological language. Both hated the same groups within society. And yet there are several important and noticeable differences. Their styles are different: Rutherford always used a pseudo-technical style overburdened with legal phrases. He never ascribed to himself the degree of scholarship claimed by Russell who spoke of knowing both Greek and Hebrew—but under oath during a trial confessed that he knew nothing of these languages.[29] Rutherford made no such claims, although he regularly used various ancient and modern translations of the Bible and various Bible helps. Of the two, Russell was the more enamored of charts and diagrams; in *Studies in the Scriptures*, he gave a considerable part of his attention to the construction of charts which attempted to graph the course of history in a systematic manner. After Russell's death, his successor also employed some charts to explain his views of history, but this practice was soon discontinued and the later official literature does not contain any such efforts.

One of Rutherford's most significant characteristics was his unwillingness to meet his followers or outsiders. Especially in his last years, he became an almost mythical personage, appearing to his followers only once or twice a year at their international conventions. The Witnesses did not know this man, their leader; they had not, for the most part, even seen him. He was apparently unwilling to be photographed extensively and he revealed nothing about his personal life. Although his secrecy had all the advantages which accrue from the mysterious, nevertheless, it was a practice which failed to instill confidence and to create among the Witnesses any real feeling of oneness with their leader. To them he was largely a written page. His last years of leadership differed greatly

[28] Rutherford, *Judge Rutherford Uncovers the Fifth Column*, pp. 3–4.
[29] Ross, *Some Facts and More Facts*, p. 18.

from the early ones in which his followers often wrote him as did one woman from Rhode Island:

Dear Judge Rutherford: I hope your cold is better soon. Your voice seemed so tired. I could hear you sigh and cough a few times Sunday. We cannot afford to have you sick; so you want to take a little rest.[30]

Toward the end of his life, his followers did not think of him in such personal terms. He was their leader, their inaccessible commander.

Mr. Rutherford's death was surrounded with as much mystery as was his life. He died on January 8, 1942, at the age of seventy-two. Few people knew he was ill, but actually it seems that his health had been poor for some time. In 1940, Mr. A. D. Schroeder, the Society's leader in England, wrote Rutherford that he was sorry to learn he was "not so well," but rejoiced that he was "slowly gaining strength." [31] In the spring of 1941 it was widely rumored among the Witnesses that there would be no international convention that year. The Witnesses felt that there must be some basis for the rumor, but just what it was they themselves did not know. The date for the last international convention at which Mr. Rutherford appeared was announced, however, in May, 1941. The announcement was made much later in the year than was usual. I heard some Witnesses say that perhaps the convention had been put off because of the health of Mr. Rutherford.

For several years before his death, Mr. Rutherford had lived at Beth-Sarim, the palatial West-coast headquarters of the Society. He retired to these comfortable surroundings and left the actual work of the organization to Mr. N. H. Knorr, the then vice president. At the Brooklyn headquarters, Mr. Rutherford was simply "out of town" during these years.

The cause of Mr. Rutherford's death was not disclosed, but Dr. George Roy Stevenson, who signed the death certificate, said Rutherford "had known for eighteen months of the malignant condition that eventually brought his death." [32] No one in the organization seemed to have anticipated his death, for no carefully prepared official statement was ever issued. The source of the news was a mortician in San Diego, California, where Beth-Sarim is located. Two days later the public learned that Rutherford's last wish had been that he be buried, not in Missouri, the state of his birth, but in a hillside crypt on the estate of Beth-Sarim. He

[30] *Watch Tower*, March, 1932.   [31] *Ibid.*, Oct., 1940.
[32] Reading (Pa.) *Eagle*, Jan. 12, 1942.

desired that his burial take place at the dawn of the day following his death. This wish seems to indicate that he wanted his death to disrupt the organization as little as possible. His burial was held up, however, because of a county law forbidding any burials outside of legally zoned cemeteries. In the meantime preparations went on to erect an elaborate memorial to Rutherford at Beth-Sarim. Five months after his death his body was finally interred at Rossville, New York.

Rutherford's death closed the second cycle in the history of the Jehovah's Witnesses. The organization which Pastor Russell founded and enlarged into a world-wide business was consolidated and augmented by the Pastor's militant successor. It has been strong enough to survive the death of Leader No. II, and to carry on.

Organization and Finances

THE WORK OF THE JEHOVAH'S WITNESSES is conducted by three corporations, formed chiefly for the purpose of holding property and publishing literature. The first of these is the Watch Tower Bible and Tract Society of Pennsylvania which was incorporated in that state as the Zion's Watch Tower Society in 1884, and provided the movement with its first official corporate status. When the Witness movement spread abroad, its missionary organization was incorporated in England in 1914 as the International Bible Students Association. This is the title generally used today to designate the work of the Society in countries other than the United States. The third organization was incorporated in New York as the People's Pulpit Association in 1909 and as the Watch Tower Bible and Tract Society in 1939.

Of the three organizations, the Pennsylvania corporation originally founded by Mr. Russell is the best known among the Witnesses themselves. In it are counted all those who have given ten dollars or more to the work. Although it maintains a mailing office in Pittsburgh, its headquarters are in Brooklyn. Its officers at the time of Rutherford's death were Joseph F. Rutherford, president, C. A. Wise, vice president, William E. Van Amburgh, secretary-treasurer.

The New York corporation consists of approximately forty members (the first group was appointed by Mr. Rutherford), most of whom are actively engaged in the management of all three organizations from the Brooklyn headquarters. This is the only one of the three bodies which may hold property. Its members elect annually a Board of Directors, usually twelve in number. At the time of Rutherford's death the members of the Board were Joseph F. Rutherford, president, Fred W. Franz, Nathan H. Knorr, vice president, Grant Suiter, T. J. Sullivan, William P. Heath, Jr., Hugo H. Riemer, William E. Van Amburgh, secretary-treasurer, Arthur R. Gaux, C. A. Wise, Clayton J. Woodworth, M. A. Howlett. The Board of Directors of the New York corporation formally holds the real authority in the movement and also controls the other two corporations. Rutherford was, however, the central figure on the Board and dominated its every decision.

Thus the set-up of the controlling corporation is similar to that of an ecclesiastical autocracy. In the fall of 1941, one of the former "higher-ups" wrote in a letter to me:

Rutherford controls the organization completely. Directors and members meetings are a formality. The Judge sends a note stating whom he wants elected, or rejected, or what he wants done, and that is immediately done unanimously. Woe be unto that one who opposes. Anyone that opposes slightly gets a tongue lashing at the dinner table, and if the opposition is serious, or such one has too much independence of mind he is liquidated from the organization.[1]

Little is known of the personal history of any of the Board members. They obscure their personal responsibilities and appear in public little more than did Mr. Rutherford. They are in charge, however, of some important departments of the work of the Society. Mr. N. H. Knorr was general manager of the printing plant in Brooklyn, and thus pre-eminently responsible for the management of a factory employing nearly two hundred Witnesses in the manufacture of official literature. As vice president of the Board, he spoke for the Society whenever Mr. Rutherford was absent, and after Rutherford's death assumed supreme command of the total organization until he was elected president in the spring of 1942. Mr. Knorr steadfastly refused to confer with anyone "merely seeking information" about the Society, although, on the other hand, he offered to come personally to my home if I was "really interested in the truth."

Mr. Gaux was entrusted with some of the minor legal matters of the Society. He impressed me as less interested in these matters, or even in matters of general knowledge, than in seeking converts. Although a member of the Board of Directors, he was merely an assistant to Mr. Covington, the head counsel of the Society who later became vice president as well.

In the early years of the movement the members of the Board of the Pennsylvania corporation were elected annually by the whole membership, but as early as 1925 the election was made triennial, a practice in force today. Board members of the Pennsylvania corporation have always been nominated and elected from the membership of the New York corporation. In actual practice, membership on the Pennsylvania Board is restricted to those who comprise the New York Board. Thus the voting of the Witnesses has consistently followed the desires of Mr. Rutherford and his close associates. Usually the directors are considered by the Witnesses to have life tenure upon the Board. I cannot recall any

---

[1] Name of the writer withheld by request.

director having been defeated in an election, if he chose to run for another term. This means that the management of the Jehovah's Witnesses is entrusted to a small group of men whose leadership for the most part is unquestioned over rather long periods of time.

In this regard, criticism of the Society by individual Witnesses is believed to be a form of blasphemy: "Many find fault with the Society, its officers and organization, but in their hearts generally it is the Lord they are rejecting." [2]

The Society, moreover, is considered by all Witnesses to be God-ordained, depending upon men in no manner. Its decisions are taken as divinely inspired and obligatory upon all true believers: "Who can doubt that the Lord of the harvest is at the helm and steering Zion homeward through the instrumentality of the Watch Tower Bible and Tract Society, the only divine repository?" [3] Or, as another letter puts it: "The Society, and it alone, is the custodian of the great Divine plan." [4]

Even the change from annual to triennial election of Board members failed to alarm the pious believer, since the whole organization is in the keeping of Jehovah. A Witness from California testifies:

Since coming to understand the truth I have recognized the fact that while the Church has the privilege of appointing its elders and officers, the Lord himself arranged for the Laodicean Servant, the Watch Tower Bible and Tract Society, and its present officers. This it seems is solely the Lord's prerogative. I feel, therefore, as a member of his Body, that I am wonderfully privileged to receive food at the Lord's table. Not only food but directions as to the carrying out of the will of the Lord, and entering into his joy.[5]

Since the Society is connected so closely with what it considers to be divine, its program is not to be thwarted by any individuals or groups, particularly of Witnesses. One local group wrote Mr. Rutherford that it had doubted the wisdom of conducting meetings in the manner prescribed by the central organization, but after due consideration became "convinced that the Society's way is the best, and [we] wish to be in harmony with it." [6]

The fact that the Witnesses are not called upon to participate in a genuinely democratic organization seems in general to please them. The primary task of the individual believer is to trust and to trust again. He does not need to think about the running of the movement. He does

---

[2] *Watch Tower*, March, 1935.   [3] *Ibid.*, May, 1925.   [4] *Ibid.*, June, 1925.
[5] *Ibid.*   [6] *Ibid.*, April, 1925.

not have to share in formulating its policies or in creating new modes of action. All things come from the Society, and to the Society each individual believer owes his soul. This type of religious experience is sought eagerly by many who, upon conversion, become a docile variety of Witness. To them the Society, not the Bible, is the final source of inspiration. One Witness glories in the fact that "the blessing which we receive through the Society is even greater than ever before." [7] A leader of a local group told me that he was not interested in the "higher-ups" in the Society; he was merely interested in receiving their instructions and in carrying them out accurately.

This unchallenging attitude permitted control of the organization to pass into the hands of a few powerful leaders. When the organization held its first meeting in 1884, Mr. Russell was elected to the presidency. Until his death, in 1916, no one ever successfully challenged his right to that office. He grouped others about him to aid in caring for the rising young movement; often he gave them a substantial role to play in the creation of policies and beliefs; always he was interested in what others thought. But, after Russell's death, and from that time until Rutherford's death, a growing amalgamation of power came into the hands of fewer and fewer Witnesses. Gradually and persistently the number of unofficial Witnesses asked to express their views has grown smaller. If a Witness voiced an opinion at variance with that of the central organization he was "Satan-inspired" and was subsequently cut off from the fellowship of "true believers." This procedure applied even to duly elected chairmen of local groups. More and more the leadership gravitated into the hands of one person, Mr. Rutherford, so that by the time of his death the entire organization, including the Board of Directors, was controlled by this one man.

One day in 1941, I telephoned the Society's headquarters to obtain some information from its head counsel, Mr. Covington. He said that he was unable to disclose the information which I sought. When I asked him from whom it might be obtained, he answered, "From the Society." I quickly replied, "And who is the Society?" After some hesitation he ventured, "Ask Judge Rutherford." I have found consistently that few Witnesses either "high" or "low" (in terms of their intimate relationship to the central organization) care to answer any question or make any statement as to the inner structure of the Society.

[7] *Ibid.*

The opinion of Mr. Czatt, a student who made a study of the Jehovah's Witnesses, to the effect that "Judge Rutherford has shown himself to be a very able executive," is far from an overstatement.[8] Rutherford, too, was an *Oberste Befehlshaber der Wehrmacht* (Supreme Commander of the Army). A leader of a house meeting where the writings of Mr. Rutherford were studied repeatedly said, when making announcements, that he had "orders" to say what he did. Increasingly, in recent years, the organization has taken on the character of a secret society.

Attached to the Society is a legal staff to aid Witnesses who have been persecuted or jailed. The legal department handles such matters as the relation of Witnesses to the Selective Service Act, flag saluting, and the problems of those who refuse public school education. Mr. Covington, as head of the department, traveled incessantly to near and distant parts of the country for trials involving Witnesses. In a courtroom, during a case, I have heard Witnesses say of Covington that he was "smart," that he certainly was a devout Witness (which to them made considerable difference in the quality of a man), and that he was a hard worker.

Before his election as vice president, Mr. Covington was head counsel for five years. His predecessor, Mr. Olin R. Moyle, was dismissed on August 8, 1939, by the Board of Directors "by reason of his unfaithfulness to the kingdom interests and to those who serve the kingdom." The background of his "unfaithfulness" seems to have been a letter which he wrote to protest some faults in the organization as he saw them. The letter, although addressed to Rutherford, was written to all at the central office in Brooklyn.[9] It revealed Moyle's opinion of the living conditions at Bethel House, where many of the full-time workers of the organization "keep house" coöperatively, and of the way in which Mr. Rutherford conducted his personal relations with the Witnesses. Four complaints were listed: Rutherford's frequent scoldings and upbraidings of the workers at Bethel House; discrimination by Rutherford against his followers in favor of himself in the matter of comforts and conveniences; excessive use of alcohol at Bethel; and overindulgence in vulgar language there.

Substantiating the first complaint, Moyle cited several concrete cases, among them, one involving Witnesses who were ushers at a meeting in Madison Square Garden in New York City.[10] Concerning the charge

[8] Milton Stacey Czatt, *The International Bible Students*, p. 6.
[9] A copy of the letter was given me by Mr. Moyle.   [10] See p. 153.

of discrimination, Moyle stated that Rutherford, although preaching that all in "the Lord's organization" were treated alike by the Society, lived in luxury while many of his workers were denied the comforts and sometimes the necessities of life. Rutherford was charged with having various homes throughout the country, and it was claimed that a house on the Kingdom Farm in New York was reserved for his sole use.

In regard to the third charge, Moyle wrote that drinking was not only permitted but even encouraged at Bethel; those who did not drink liquor lost "caste" with the Society's officials. Those who entered Bethel as abstainers were looked upon as neophytes, for whom a systematic approach was engineered for further "conversion." Finally, Moyle suggested that many at Bethel House were prone to use vulgar language. He stated that the loudest laughter at the dining table came with the telling of filthy jokes, and in this respect Rutherford himself was not innocent.

Moyle never wished to sever his relations with the movement, but was desirous of reforming certain evils of official practice and of communal life at Bethel House. The Board, however, could not tolerate such criticism and dismissed Moyle without a hearing. At the time of his dismissal, Moyle's son was loyal to his father, but later renounced him and recognized the Society as the true determiner of right and wrong conduct.

Upon his dismissal, Moyle sought to return to Wisconsin, where he had previously practiced law, and there to take up private practice anew, while still remaining within the Witness movement. Mr. Rutherford, however, excommunicated him from all meetings and activities of the organization. In the fall of 1942 Mr. Moyle entered suit against Rutherford and the other members of the Board of Directors for statements which he called libelous. The case came to trial late in 1944 and was decided in Mr. Moyle's favor; he was awarded $25,000 damages.

There are numerous ways in which the Witnesses are ruled by the officials of the Society. Each year thousands of Witnesses gather at an international convention to hear the latest word from the leader and to engage in mass distribution of the literature. The origin of these conventions dates back to 1893 when the first, attended by 360 believers, was held in Chicago during August (the month in which train fares were lowest).[11] It was here that the practice of baptism was introduced. For some time the early assemblies were called "Believers' Conventions."

[11] *Watch Tower*, July, 1893.

During the latter part of Mr. Russell's life, several conventions were held in various parts of the United States so that Witnesses from every section would have opportunity to attend. In one year sectional meetings were held in Boston and St. Louis. When the movement spread, conventions were held in other countries until, under the leadership of Mr. Rutherford, the Society introduced "International Conventions." In past years such gatherings have been held in Paris, London, Toronto, New York, and other cities.

The Society has put pressure upon the Witnesses to attend these gatherings, offering for the purpose an extra bonus (an advance on the income from future book sales) to Witnesses engaged in full-time work. In one of the local groups, just after a convention had been announced, I heard the leader urge all to attend; he implied that any who did not were "doubtful members of the Body of Christ." The announcement of a convention is a significant event to the Witnesses. When such an announcement (signed by Mr. Rutherford) was read in one local meeting, the whole group agreed that it denoted good news, for it meant that Jehovah had imparted to the revered leader the knowledge that the end of the age would not come at least before the convention; some even thought it might come at the time of the convention itself.

The number of attendants has risen sharply in recent years. In 1935 at the international convention held in Washington, D.C., about 20,000 were present, according to the Society's own estimate.[12] In 1941, some 115,000 met in St. Louis, and in 1942, in Cleveland, the number was 83,894. At the Cleveland convention there were over a thousand ushers. The usual procedure for the ushers is to carry canes, for the Witnesses have experienced in the past the wrath of certain community groups who feel that the movement is a menace to established religion and fiery patriotism. Even Mr. Rutherford and his close assistants were in the habit of carrying canes at these meetings. During the convention in Newark, New Jersey, in 1937, 120 Witnesses were locked securely in jail twenty-four to forty-eight hours before the convention began; sixty-six were detained until the convention had closed, because the city authorities considered them an active threat to the peace.[13] Witnesses generally wear badges so that they can easily recognize each other in a crowd.

Occasionally Mr. Rutherford encountered difficulties in securing a place of meeting. This has been especially true in recent years after the

[12] *Yearbook*, 1935.   [13] Rutherford, *Armageddon*, p. 29.

Witnesses had incurred the antagonism of various religious and patriotic groups. The Witnesses, however, have always paid their bills, and businessmen of the convention cities have spoken favorably of the manner in which they conduct themselves. For example, the city of Columbus, Ohio, proffered Rutherford the use of the Fair Grounds for July 24–28, 1940, largely because the Witness convention in that city three years earlier had met with obvious success for the businessmen. The invitation was accepted and a contract for the Fair Grounds was signed by the Society and the State Fair Association. But, later, the Fair management, believing that the convention would cause a "disturbance," canceled the contract. Rutherford accused the management of being influenced by Bishop Hartley, the "Reverend Father" Murphy, and the Knights of Columbus, all of whom were local Catholics hated by the Witnesses.[14] Faithful Witnesses from all parts of the country were organized to gather several million signatures which they sent in a petition to Governor Bricker of Ohio that he might formally recognize their right to assemble. However, the Governor, like the Fair Association, was adamant, and new arrangements for the convention had to be made with another city. After lengthy deliberations, Detroit, Michigan, agreed to receive the Witnesses.

The Detroit convention was typical of many in recent years. Close to fifty thousand Witnesses flocked to the city during four days of mid-August heat. They came from all parts of this country and some few from other lands. When the Witnesses reached the meeting place they were assembled and classified into various squads for active, door-to-door canvassing. They handed out over a million items of their literature to people within a fifty-mile radius of Detroit. Daily they listened to reports of the year's progress from Witness leaders and twice, once at the beginning and again at the close of the convention, heard Mr. Rutherford speak "in person."

Where Rutherford lived while he was in Detroit was known to a few of his closest friends only. He was not available to ordinary Witnesses for personal conference and did not remain after the meetings for discussion. He came promptly into the meeting hall at the appointed time, delivered his speech (copies of which were immediately handed to the assembled Witnesses for distribution to the people of Detroit), and was whisked away. At each convention it was Mr. Rutherford's custom to

[14] Rutherford, *Judge Rutherford Uncovers the Fifth Column*, pp. 24 ff.

introduce a resolution that would subsequently be passed with great enthusiasm. In general, the resolutions merely described some condition or hope with which the Witnesses had long been acquainted.

The fervor of the Witnesses was doubtless increased by the various "props" employed during the meetings. The defensive canes which Mr. Rutherford, his assistants, and the ushers have generally carried, caused a certain tenseness. According to the personal report of a number of Witnesses, once when the convention was held in New Jersey the stage from which Mr. Rutherford spoke was lined with machine guns, purportedly for his protection from the Roman Catholic Hierarchy. The Witnesses at this meeting were brought to a frenzy over the idea that their leader needed to be protected with machine guns from an invading squad of armed priests. Several Witnesses told me that guards were stationed by Rutherford on the roof of the meeting hall in Detroit to report any airplane which came over, because it had been rumored—and many Witnesses believed it—that enemies of the movement had banded together and were planning to bomb the place while Mr. Rutherford was speaking.

Usually the conventions have been linked by telephone with other Witness meetings throughout the world. For example, while the Detroit assembly was in progress, 3,500 Witnesses convened in Manchester, England. The group there had its own local business to transact, but the program focused on Mr. Rutherford's speeches in Detroit. At the same time, all over the world wherever they were able to assemble, Witnesses were holding simultaneous conventions. This procedure has worked out advantageously, especially since the outbreak of the second World War, because many countries could not be represented if a truly international convention were called at one place. Usually the smaller conventions follow the program of the central meeting.

Until recently Negro Witnesses were barred from the official conventions but were encouraged to hold separate ones of their own. As the reason for this, Witnesses have cited the fact that many of the Negroes live in the South and cannot afford the long and costly journey to the convention city; they are therefore free to meet in a place more readily accessible to them. This does not seem a completely valid excuse, however, for at least one of the Negro conventions was held at Atlantic City, New Jersey. Apparently Mr. Rutherford never appeared at these Negro conventions.

To facilitate the management of its vast enterprise in this country and to provide for the greatest possible efficiency among its workers, territorial and organizational divisions of the Society have been made. Thus, the United States has been divided into six major regions consisting of 154 zones, which in turn are composed of innumerable local companies. Controlling each of these divisions is a representative appointed by the Society. The six major regions are managed by a "regional servant" who is responsible only to the Board of Directors. The regional servants must be loyal, skilled in the management of the Society's work, and capable of producing the required results. They make few personal contacts with local groups, but work mainly through their "zone servants."

Each zone servant controls many local groups. His job is to see that quotas of literature distribution assigned him by his regional servant are met by the local groups in his charge. Occasionally he visits his local groups and "inspects" them. During these inspections, of several days duration, he spends his time auditing the group's financial records, chastizing or praising the local leaders, and holding private conferences with any Witnesses who feel the need of his advice. Sometimes, but not necessarily, he is asked to lead a local meeting. His coming is heralded by the Witnesses in several ways: some anticipate his visit as an official recognition of the success of their efforts; others feel that it means a "time of account-taking" when their efforts will be scrutinized critically, not only by the zone servant but also by the local leader. The inspection by the zone servant usually results in an unwelcome increase in the group's literature quotas.

Sometimes the zone servant calls "zone assemblies," which are scheduled usually for an entire week end. A large part of the program is devoted to a concerted effort to canvass the particular area of the city in which the assembly is being held. In the afternoons and evenings of each day, the zone servant and other leaders instruct newly converted Witnesses in the proper methods of distributing the literature. Frequently, baptism is administered to new converts. A recorded speech by Mr. Rutherford closes the zone assembly.

The local group, called "the Company," corresponds in many ways to a church congregation. In 1943 there were 3,421 of these companies.[15] The name "Company" is a remnant of the older military classification of the various services and divisions of the organization. Formerly the

[15] *Yearbook*, 1943.

zone servant was called "the Captain"; members with special duties in the local groups were also sometimes called "Captains," and even to-day some of them are termed "Lieutenants." Although Witnesses of the rank and file frequently assumed such titles as "soldier," "battler," and the like, their usual present-day practice is to address each other as "brother" and "sister."

The local place of meeting is called a "Kingdom Hall," for the Witnesses never apply the term "church" to their meeting place. Halls are rented from various organizations—the Elks, the Odd Fellows, or some other group (with whom the Witnesses would otherwise not be associated). If no suitable hall is available, space is rented in a factory or office building. The numerical basis upon which a local group is formed is an attendance of about two hundred at the Sunday evening meetings. Company leaders have told me that if a group succeeds in attracting more than that number, a new Company is formed and some of the Witnesses are assigned to the new meeting place. In 1943, 244 new Companies were formed.[16]

The highest office in a Company is that of the "service director." In an especially large Company there may also be an "assistant service director." Theoretically the service director and his assistant, if there is one, are elected by the local Company for a term of one year, but actually the local group does not elect anyone whom the central organization has not first approved. The position of service director may be permanent, for as long as he pleases the central organization his election in the local group is assured. The service director is responsible ultimately to the Society, but immediately to the zone servant, for the running of the local group.

Other officers who are elected by the Company members comprise what is known as the "service committee." These Witnesses have various and not wholly related jobs to do. One member of the service committee is in charge of "back-calls," another is in charge of reports, and so on. The committee members work independently of each other and are responsible only to the service director.

There is also a "chairman" in every local group, whose duty is to conduct the meetings. This officer is usually not the service director, although there is no rule against the holding of two offices by one person at the same time. Ordinarily the service director is not a member of the local

[16] *Ibid.*

community but is sent by the Brooklyn headquarters to manage the Company's affairs and to stimulate the Witnesses to greater service. The chairman of the Company, on the other hand, is a member of the local community; as such, he is in daily contact with the individual Witnesses under his jurisdiction and comes to know them well. He is therefore used by the service director to act as intermediary in various local matters. The service director, with whom the greater authority is lodged, works behind the scenes, with the chairman of the Company acting as his "front." The chairman may be changed frequently, even more often than once a year.

The Company also elects a secretary-treasurer for a period of one year, unless for a specific reason a longer term of office is advisable. The election of one person to serve as both secretary and treasurer of the Company is in accord with the practice of combining those offices in other areas of the organization; for example, in the Board of Directors of the Society. The secretary-treasurer is not directly in charge of the sale of literature, but he must make a monthly report to the central organization of the financial intake from such sales. Each Company has a "storekeeper" who directs the sale of the literature and is financially responsible to the secretary-treasurer. The post of storekeeper is also an elective one, but does not carry the prestige of the other offices.

The position of women in the local organization is one of almost complete subordination to the men. No women are prominent in the higher ranks of leadership. They are admitted as believers and often answer questions in the meetings of the local group but are seldom consulted in business matters and are practically never elected to office. In fact, the Society officially declared that women are to be tolerated in the Company but are not to be encouraged to seek office.[17]

The organization of the Jehovah's Witnesses is charted.

From this chart, the autocratic nature of the organization is evident.

The Company meetings are conducted with little ritual or liturgy, as commonly conceived. The nature of the meeting places precludes the use of stained-glass windows, regular pews, chancels, and so on, but their absence is not considered a loss. A typical meeting room is barren except for the symbols or decorations of the organizations from whom the hall is rented, and for slogans put up by the Witnesses, such as "Religion is Doomed" or "Thy Word is Truth." Charts are hung on the walls to

[17] *Watch Tower*, June, 1928.

explain the progress of the Company in terms of the hours spent in canvassing houses, the number of pamphlets, books, and magazines sold, and the number of back-calls made. In addition, the charts compare the present efforts of the group with those of the previous month and year.

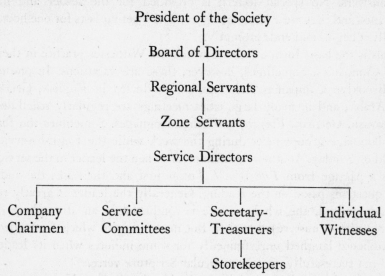

President of the Society

Board of Directors

Regional Servants

Zone Servants

Service Directors

Company Chairmen — Service Committees — Secretary-Treasurers — Individual Witnesses

Storekeepers

   Meetings are opened and closed with prayer. The prayers of the Witnesses differ only in minor respects from those of members of the traditional churches. They are directed to "Our Heavenly Father" and not to "Jehovah," and close with the phrase "in Jesus' name,"—one of the few occasions on which the name of Jesus is mentioned. The leader frequently calls upon members of the audience to offer prayer. The prayers are usually petitions to God for peace and contentment, recovery from illness, strength for work, and vision for the truth. The believers seldom pray for the Society's leader and never for those other than Witnesses. Few Witnesses close their eyes during prayer at these meetings, and none kneel. The Witnesses usually sit during prayer except at the end of the meeting when it is customary for them to stand.

   The leader opens the meeting by asking a series of questions received from the central organization. The questions are based upon the material in the current issue of *The Watch Tower*. The people in the audience who think they can answer raise their hands and are called upon. After several Witnesses have given their views, the leader calls upon an assistant to read the corresponding passage in *The Watch Tower*, which answers the question according to the point of view of the Society. Thus, all "imperfect" answers are corrected and the Witnesses obediently listen to the reading of the magazine as to a voice "from on high." Sometimes the leader has two assistants, one to read the questions, the other to read the answers. No special lectern is provided for the leader and his assistants, and they wear no unique garb. The meeting lasts for one hour; usually it begins and ends promptly.

This is the basic form of service which the Witnesses practice in their local Companies. Sometimes, however, there are variations. In one of the Brooklyn Companies, meetings are conducted in English, Greek, and Arabic, and in many large cities meetings are regularly scheduled in Spanish, German, French, and other languages. Sometimes the foreign language groups meet during the week while the English service is held on Sunday. Another variation occurs when the leader in the service reads a passage from *The Watch Tower* first and then asks the audience questions based on the reading. Generally the leader is greatly respected; indeed, the whole service is conducted in an atmosphere of sincere (almost austere) devotion. But in one service which I attended, the audience laughed unrestrainedly for some minutes when its leader could not successfully quote a particular Scripture verse.

In many Companies, especially in the Northern states, Negroes are as welcome as whites; they tend to sit together and to recognize one of their brethren as spokesman, while the whites tend to gravitate toward each other and to assume the administrative functions. Only in the Negro sections of large cities and in the South are there local Companies almost completely under the control of Negroes. In Harlem, New York City, one Company of Witnesses has several Negroes among its officers, but it also has a few Puerto Ricans and a white service director. A number of local Companies are led by Jewish service directors who are praised by Gentile Witnesses for their "organizing abilities."

In some Companies difficulties arise—infrequently over color differences—that cause considerable strife among the members. In the event of a problem, the service director handles the situation unless he himself is involved, in which case the zone servant seeks to straighten out the difficulty. Sometimes the central organization has been called in to solve the difficulty.[18]

[18] *Ibid.*, May, 1914.

The second World War has had the effect of making the Company more than ever a closed group to which outsiders are "foreigners." Before the declaration of war, I was asked occasionally by Witnesses whether I were a Roman Catholic priest in disguise, a newspaperman, or a representative of the American Legion seeking information. Since the declaration, I have been carefully scrutinized and interrogated as to whether I was a member of the Federal Bureau of Investigation, sent as a government "spy." One leader in a colored Company (fearing I was a representative of the F.B.I.) said that he was worried all through the meeting that I might misconstrue some remark of his and put him in jail. After the close of another meeting, the leader quelled the fears of the group by assuring them that I did not represent the government. On still another occasion, a group of Witnesses insisted upon accompanying me for several blocks in order to ask me about my background and the reasons for my strange interest in Witnesses. Throughout my study of the Witnesses my activities were reported to the central organization, so that when I finally sought out one of the Board of Directors he knew of every visit I had made and every proposal I had submitted to a local Company. At the present time, the Witnesses feel themselves to be under surveillance because of their refusal to support any government in the war. In the face of outward calamity, they have reëmphasized their separation from the rest of the community, have withdrawn into the fellowship of the like-minded, and have defined less permeable boundaries around their corporate life.

The finances of the local Company are quite small in view of the amount of literature distributed and the frequency of meetings. No collection is taken up, although at the rear of every meeting place there is a wooden box for voluntary offerings. The Witnesses are told repeatedly that the Society is "not run for profit" and that "the Lord will take care of his people." The movement is said by its followers not to be interested in worldly things, and yet I have seldom been in a Company meeting where the need of money has not been stressed. The leader regrets that he must mention the subject because doing so is a sign of a Satan-controlled organization, and yet he must.

The biggest item of expense is that of rent for the meeting place (sometimes including small attached offices). This varies according to the locality, but seldom exceeds $125 per month (the figure in New York City).

The following is the balance sheet of a Brooklyn Company for a normal month:

Balance for August: $46.[a]

Receipts for September:

Contributions	$154.
Sale of Bibles	9.
Use of telephone	2.
Telephone calls by individuals	.45
Receipts for "The Watch Tower"	30.
Receipts for "Consolation"	27.
Receipts for books and pamphlets	181.
Receipts for records	137.
Check cashed	23.
Total about	$610.

Expenses for September:

Rent	$100.
Telephone	7.
Electric light	3.
Bible account	3.
Window cleaning	2.
Cardboard separators	.45
"The Watch Tower"	30.
"Consolation"	27.
Books and pamphlets	181.
Records	137.
Check cashed	23.
Total about	$510.

Balance for September: about $100.
Petty cash balance: about $9.

[a] All figures are simply in terms of dollars; no cents are recorded unless the item is less than one dollar. The figures and entries are presented here just as they were given at the Company meeting.

At many of the Company meetings in the vicinity of Witness-owned farms, eggs and cheese are sold. In New York City these farm products are brought approximately one hundred miles for the exclusive patronage of the Witnesses at Company meetings. The Witnesses enjoy buying them because they believe they are not only helping their own organization but that they are also getting these products fresher and cheaper than they would at their local stores. Eggs and cheese are not the first or the only products that have been sold by the Society in Company meetings. In 1913, a cure for cancer was sold only to those "in the truth." [19] The famed "Millennial Bean" was an earlier offering—a bean seed which Witnesses were promised would outgrow all other varieties of beans. Later, the "Wonderful Cotton Seed" was guaranteed to "revolutionize" the production of cotton. The Society has also sold through the Companies a cure for appendicitis. In advertising the "wonder-working" product "Santonine," *The Watch Tower* said:

It is known that only about three out of every one hundred operated on for appendicitis really have a diseased appendix needing removal. We give below a simple cure for appendicitis symptoms. The pain in the appendix is caused by the biting of worms near the juncture of the transverse colon with the small intestines, low down on the right side of the abdomen. . . .

This remedy is recommended also for typhoid fever which is also a worm disease. The medicine is Santonine: dose, three grains an hour before breakfast, repeated for four mornings or until symptoms disappear. Then, one dose per month for three months to eradicate all germs.

The recipe is of incalculable value. Not only will it save the surgeon's and hospital fees of perhaps $200., but it saves weeks of ill health, inconvenience, convalescence and loss of salary.[20]

Mr. Russell was well known for his sale of "Miracle Wheat," which he predicted would produce two hundred bushels per acre as an average yield, with a possible yield of two hundred and fifty bushels. It was sold by the Society through the local groups for $60 a bushel, and, according to the accounts given in the official magazines, not enough of the seed could be obtained to meet the demand.

Aside from conventions, zone assemblies, and the local meetings (which the Witnesses call "Watch Tower Meetings"), the Society also sponsors Model Study Meetings. These are centered in a catechetical approach to the theological framework of the movement. It is uncommon in so youthful a religion for a catechetical stress to develop. Usually a religion passes through a long period of expansion in which, beginning with a few converts and meager property, it seeks widespread social acceptance and increased wealth. If a religion is able to gain such acceptance with concomitant wealth, it may mitigate the driving compulsion of its earlier stage and drift into a secure self-sufficiency in which it may be chiefly concerned with conserving what it has already gained. When a religion

[19] *Ibid.*, July, 1913.   [20] *Ibid.*, Jan., 1912.

comes to this point, it may find that it can conveniently conserve itself in part by using a catechism. Mr. Rutherford early seized upon the catechetical technique as an efficient means of enforcing unity of thought, and it does so serve.

Model Study Meetings are often held an hour before the Sunday evening Watch Tower Meetings, which they resemble, except that the subject matter for discussion is limited to three pamphlets, Model Study, Nos. 1, 2, and 3. The pamphlets contain brief questions and answers on subjects of significance especially to newly admitted Witnesses. The following is a sample passage:

Q. What warning did Paul give concerning the traditions of men?
A. Colossians 2:8; Galatians 1:8.
Q. Who was Saul's guide when he was a religionist?
A. The Devil was his guide, as is shown by what he did. I Timothy 1:13; Romans 6:16.
Q. How has the teaching of "purgatory" affected many sincere persons?
A. It has turned many away from God and his Truth, keeping them from learning of Jehovah's gracious purposes and bringing them into bondage to Satan's representatives through fear.
Q. If Satan is responsible for misleading the people, does that exonerate the Roman Hierarchy?
A. No; because they have been WILLINGLY ignorant. 2 Peter 3:5.[21]

Besides the Model Study Meetings, house meetings are also held. These are of two types: one which the Society sponsors for Witnesses and which is held each week in the homes of Witnesses; and one which is started for the instruction of initiates and is held in their own or in Witness homes. The first type of house meeting is conducted very much as are the Watch Tower Meetings, except that the questions are customarily based on one of the books written by Mr. Rutherford, rather than on *The Watch Tower*. The meeting lasts for an hour, but occasionally refreshments are served and the group lingers to discuss experiences in the field. (Witnesses report 5,593 individual locations for such meetings in 1943.)

The second type of house meeting comes about more spontaneously, as described in the report of a Witness:

Sometime ago I visited a family, and the lady from the apartment above happened to be there. She is Catholic. She complained that try as hard as she

[21] Model Study. No. 1, p. 13.

could she could not understand the Bible, and knew not why. Naturally she couldn't get any help from her priest. So I suggested that we open up a study meeting, a model study. . . . Now overjoyed at understanding the Bible, she has attended the model study ever since and has invited her two strictly Catholic sisters and others to study, who in turn have become much interested in the Truth. There are about fifteen now who attend this study, and the Lord has blessed them richly with the knowledge of the truth which is appreciated by them all. They have obtained many of our books and many subscribe for "The Watch Tower" and "Consolation," and some have already taken part in field service.[22]

Both types provide intimate contacts between more experienced Witnesses and those who have just embraced "the truth." In some places, one weekday evening is devoted to the instruction of Witnesses who are experienced and reliable enough to start field work. In this meeting "practical hints" are often given by the service director as to the most successful techniques of distributing the literature.

The Witnesses are not directly compelled to give financial support to the central organization in Brooklyn, but the Society is maintained in large part by the proceeds from the sale of literature. Although the Witnesses claim they make nothing from these sales, their opponents have accused the Society of taking exorbitant profits. Indeed, the finances of the Society have in recent years been one of the chief points of attack by outsiders. It has been charged that Mr. Rutherford himself took excessive royalties from the sales of his writings. This Mr. Rutherford emphatically denied. Concerning his writings he said:

Books are copyrighted in my name and the copyright transferred to the Watch Tower Bible and Tract Society, the only consideration being that the publications be put in the hands of the people at the least possible cost. I do not receive any royalty whatsoever.[23]

Ostensibly Mr. Rutherford received for his efforts, as do all full-time Witnesses, simply ten dollars per month, room, board, and necessary expenses.

In 1940, a writer for the New York *Evening Post* took copies of Mr. Rutherford's writings to a prominent New York City publisher to have him appraise the cost of production. The publisher said that he could sell the Society's twenty-five cent books for eleven cents and the five cent

[22] *Watch Tower*, Jan., 1939.
[23] Rutherford, *Judge Rutherford Uncovers the Fifth Column*, p. 20.

pamphlets for two cents and still realize a nominal profit. When these findings were published the cry of critics of the movement became a tumult, for here, they felt, was conclusive proof of monstrous profiteering. To these insistent critics, Mr. Rutherford replied:

Why do not the "Post" and other like publications ask the Roman Catholic Hierarchy to publish their balance sheet and to inform the public what they do with the vast sums of money they collect for saying prayers for the dead, and all the money they get by other means? . . . The Watch Tower Bible and Tract Society is not interested in what the Hierarchy do with their money. We will try to attend to our own affairs which the Lord has given us. . . . The "Post" is not anxious for the truth. . . . There is no other institution on earth or that ever has been on earth that does as much work as this Society with so small a sum of money, because there is no one in the organization who desires to make personal pecuniary profit out of such work or anything connected with it.[24]

This explanation, however, did not satisfy all of the critics, and the Society still enjoys the intense dislike of many who think it "a secret, crooked bunch who are in it for the money."

While there are no exact figures on the subject, still it seems probable that the largest part of the Society's income is derived from the sales of literature. The sums of money that pour into the central headquarters from this source comprise a sort of revolving fund used mainly to print more literature. Without a doubt some of the remainder is used to carry on the Society's other functions. Concerning the amount spent on "expenses" other than printing, the Society has remained entirely silent.

At the time of the annual business meeting Mr. Russell always gave a yearly report of the Society's financial condition, which was later published in the official magazines. During the early years of the movement's history the annual budget did not exceed $15,000. In 1898 it had reached $40,000, which fact was heralded by Russell as a special sign that God was blessing the movement. By the time of his death the movement had prospered to such an extent that its annual intake rose to approximately $200,000. During the unstable interlude which ended with the election of Rutherford, the income diminished to about $149,000, but by the early twenties it had risen again to about $200,000 and thereafter slowly increased to almost $250,000—the latest figure made public, in 1935. Since then the Society has chosen not to publish its financial record.

[24] Rutherford, *The Theocracy*, pp. 59–60.

Although tested Witnesses are told that "the books" are always open to them, to my knowledge none has ever asked to see them. Such a request would immediately mark the Witness as a doubter. The books are not open to the inspection of any outsider on the grounds that the information obtained from them would only be used by opponents to harm the organization. Obviously, no accurate or even detailed discussion of the Society's finances is possible. Several insights concerning the finances of the Jehovah's Witnesses may, however, be noted.

What are the sources of the Society's income? A substantial amount is received from individual contributors. Although Witnesses are definitely not in the higher income brackets, they are devoted souls, willing to share their small earnings with the Society in the faith that they are doing the will of Jehovah. Occasionally, however, the Society has friends who can afford to make a substantial contribution:

With a heart full of thankfulness to God for "his marvelous light," Brother Hay visited us, looked into the work, and said, "Brother, I want to have a share in this work. By simple living I can spare $10,000, and I want you to have it to put it into the service in spreading the 'harvest' message of divine love and wisdom to others who are yet in darkness, from which God has so graciously delivered me. Not only do I believe that this is the truth, but more, I believe it to be the very message ordained of God 'to gather together his elect' unto himself preparatory to the glorification with him." [25]

Another source of income is the property deeded to the Society by individual Witnesses. One woman who owned ten acres of land four miles from St. Petersburg, Florida, offered to contribute the land to the Society, for she had "no desire to withhold the land from those who wish it." [26] Another wrote:

I have concluded to furnish some means by which others better qualified may be better able to carry forward the work. I own two eighty-acre tracts of unimproved land in southern Illinois [Jefferson County]. It is my wish that this land should be sold. Accordingly I have deeded these one hundred and sixty acres of land to you, and desire that you sell them to the best possible advantage and use the proceeds to your best judgment. [27]

To what amount the Society has benefited from legacies it has never revealed. Nor has it admitted the extent of its ownership of property, and this fact alone has caused some observers to be suspicious of its

[25] *Watch Tower*, Dec., 1896.   [26] *Ibid.*, Sept., 1896.   [27] *Ibid.*, April, 1895.

basic financial honesty. Mr. Rutherford, in a letter to Mr. Malcolm Logan of the New York *Evening Post,* gave the official description of the Society's ownership of property in the following terse reply: "In answer to your questions about the money of the Watch Tower Bible and Tract Society, we own a small amount of property, which is mortgaged." To have extracted this much was an achievement, yet obviously the statement tells nothing; indeed, even Witnesess do not consider it adequate. Many have told me strongly that they wished Mr. Rutherford had published a complete financial statement (including all of the properties belonging to the Society) so that the many present misunderstandings might be ended.

The Society does publicly own a tract of land and a building known as "Beth-Sarim," in San Diego, California. According to a number of Witnesses, this property has been assessed for about $60,000. The Hebrew words "Beth-Sarim" mean "House of the Princes." The purpose of the house, which in fact is a luxurious mansion, is to serve as

some tangible proof that there are those on earth today who fully believe God and Christ Jesus and in his faithful kingdom, and who believe that the faithful men of old will soon be resurrected by the Lord, be back on the earth, and take charge of the visible affairs of earth.[28]

Title to the property is vested in the Watch Tower Bible and Tract Society, in trust for the "faithful men of old." Since the Society teaches strongly that a host of Old Testament heroes, including Abraham, Isaac, Jacob, David, and others, will return to set up the righteous kingdom of Jehovah, it has felt obligated to manifest its faith by preparing a mansion for the expected occupants before they arrive. This was done in 1929. In the meantime, rather than let the building stand idle, the past president of the Society and his assistants have used it as their West-coast headquarters. To those who doubted the purpose of the building, Mr. Rutherford replied: "You may soon meet Abraham, Daniel, and other like faithful men, who shall be here as perfect men acting as governors of the new world." [29]

Beth-Sarim displeases many Witnesses who consider it an extravagant waste of money which should have gone into more productive work and who are not yet convinced by a debatable biblical interpretation that the expense is justified. Some have told me that they wondered why Mr.

[28] Rutherford, *Salvation,* p. 311.   [29] *Consolation,* Nov., 1941.

Rutherford had not simply built himself a West-coast headquarters "and let it go at that."

The Watch Tower Bible and Tract Society also owns several radio stations. The most important, WBBR, is located in the central headquarters in Brooklyn; the transmitter is on the Society's property at Rossville, Staten Island. The program of the 1,000-watt station is available principally to residents of Brooklyn; even the better equipped receiving sets in Manhattan often cannot get the station. Each week the literature department of the Society publishes in several languages the coming week's radio program. A typical evening's entertainment is as follows:

6:00 Yiddish program
6:15 Arabic program
6:30 Dinner music: concert orchestra
7:00 Your Bible question answered: Judge Rutherford (recording)
7:05 Organ melodies: Edith White
7:30 Kingdom instructions: Lecture, "The Feast," Judge Rutherford (recording)
7:45 Musical program
8:00 Sign off

The personnel of the radio station is recruited from talented Witnesses who have been called by the Society into full-time employment in managing, producing, and executing its programs. The recorded speeches of Mr. Rutherford always figure large in the program. Before his death he occasionally spoke "in person." The money value of WBBR and other stations owned by the Society has never been made public.

The eight-floor factory in Brooklyn where the literature is published is also owned by the Society. The offices of the Jehovah's Witnesses, aside from that of the president, are located on the top floor. One enters the factory via a reception room leading to a single elevator. The reception room is manned by a Witness who bears the impress of his faith in speech and manner. His duties are to inquire the business of incoming strangers and to attend the telephone switchboard. To call upon the more influential members of the Society, one must pass the receptionist's questioning. On a table near the seats where callers wait until their appointments have been arranged, lie copies of the latest *Watch Tower* and *Consolation* and an occasional pamphlet or two.

The eighth floor, where the general offices are located, gives the impression of much activity. There is no specific person to announce a visitor.

The caller sits on a chair near the elevator until he can attract the attention of a passing Witness and ask for help. Meanwhile, all he can do is to watch the Witnesses at work. Executives mingle with the worker-Witnesses in caring for the vast volume of business which falls to them each day, or chat with callers in the open space near the elevator (a number of doors are marked "Private," and one sees few visitors pass through them). Coatless men walk about with handfuls of papers; telephones rend the air with their insistent ringing; typewriters clatter; and the hum of machinery from lower floors announces that presswork of the Jehovah's Witnesses is in progress.

On the lower floors in the factory part of the building, the workers go about their task with precision and diligence. Those I have talked with told me that they feel themselves a valuable part of the "only organization that is doing God's will." Some of them long for the time when they can become active in distributing from door to door the literature they produce, since canvassing is more "exciting" to them than the largely impersonal and routinized work of the factory. But, on the whole, they seem content in the belief that Jehovah has blessed them with special aptitudes among "all sorts needed to make the organization a success."

The factory was built in 1931 and was financed by a bond issue. For some time the magazines of the Society had regularly carried applications for bonds, but the sale did not bring enough money to cover the total cost of construction and the year 1931 closed with a deficit. So far as the public knows, 1931 is the only year that the Society did not operate on a paying basis. After the building was completed, the Society's magazines carried stories from its bondholders: some said that they were happy to make the investment because of the purpose of the building; others said that they wished to change their loan to an outright gift. There is no record as to whether the factory is now completely owned by the Society, but recently there have been no direct pleas for financial aid for the project.

The employees of the factory and some full-time distributors of the literature live near by in "Bethel House," an attractive, seven-story brick building similar in appearance to an ordinary new apartment building. Together with the factory it is reportedly valued at close to $1,000,000. Bethel House is built upon the plot of ground of the old Henry Ward Beecher mansion. In 1909, when Mr. Russell moved the headquarters of the Society to Brooklyn from Pittsburgh in order that it might be "in the hub of the world's religious activities," he was able to buy Beecher's spacious home overlooking the East River. Here the central organization was located until Bethel House was ready for occupancy in the early thirties. Bethel House contains several offices, a common dining room, laundry, shoe shop, tailor shop, and living quarters, and it provides clean, frugal living space for about two hundred workers. The rising bell sounds at 6:30 each morning and lights go out at 10:30 in the evening. Meals are served in the common dining room, where Mr. Rutherford used to eat when he was "in town." Except for occasional whispers, the Witnesses eat in silence. Mr. Rutherford used to sit behind a loudspeaker at the head of the room and through the loudspeaker the hungry Witnesses heard him speak. Words of encouragement and advice or "Please pass the bread" came with equal assurance from his lips.

The occupants of Bethel House live in what one of them told me is "a primitive Christian community." When a loyal Witness applies (on a prepared form) for a position at the factory or at Bethel House, and is accepted, he voluntarily foregoes all profitable employment. At Bethel the Society provides him with room and board and a monthly allotment for incidentals. During the lifetime of Mr. Russell the monthly allowance was $20; later it was reduced to $16, and in 1944 it was $10. The communal basis of living really began in 1891 when a few devotees of Mr. Russell, seeking to show their complete devotion to the faith, resigned their regular employment and lived together on what was given them by those who admired their action. There is no tenet in the Witness creed which even implies, however, that this practice is necessary or desirable for all true believers. Generally, Witnesses are not in sympathy with "communism," although one Witness did express the view that owning property was evil because all things belong to Jehovah. Holding this premise, he also agreed that "everybody is entitled to use everything."

According to official reports, Mr. Russell received no more pay than did the lowliest worker in his organization. His expenses were higher, but these were not counted as part of his allowance. Presumably Mr. Rutherford also worked upon the same basis, although he never gave any precise information as to his financial relationship with the Society. It is interesting to note that Mr. Russell bequeathed only $200 in his will, and this to his wife. Rutherford's will was never made public.

Some of the food for Bethel residents is provided by Witness-owned farms in New York State. The Society owns in this state about two hundred acres, which are devoted to dairy and "truck" farming. Throughout the United States, the Society owns other farms, which usually have been deeded or willed to the organization by faithful Witnesses. The workers on the farms live under the same arrangement as do those at Bethel. The farmers rejoice that "all work is the same to the Lord." It pleases them to realize that the farm foreman receives no more than the humblest laborer among them.

Among additional properties owned by the Society in other countries throughout the world is a large printing establishment in England. What the status of its property in the dictator-ruled countries is, not even the Society itself can ascertain.

Literature and Workers

EACH OF THE FOUR distinctively American religious developments relies upon the Hebrew-Christian Bible as its primary textbook of religion. To each, the Bible has different fundamental meanings, but each is zealous in appreciation of the book, and considers it the final source of authority. Of these truly American religious developments, two have followed similar patterns in expressing their relation to the Bible—Christian Science and the Jehovah's Witnesses.[1] Both of these groups have developed extensive literatures called "Bible helps." Mary Baker Eddy's *Key to the Scriptures,* a volume basic to any understanding of the Christian Science movement, was intended by its author as a guide to "the only accurate way of interpreting the Bible." With similar intent, in the movement known as the Jehovah's Witnesses there has developed a voluminous literature which purports to be the sole guide for an accurate interpretation of the Bible.

Probably the distribution of the literature of the Watch Tower Bible and Tract Society has surpassed that of any other American movement, religious or secular. The number of items of reading matter distributed from door to door in any recent year makes the sales of "best sellers" look like census figures on small towns. The Witnesses believe that anyone can learn the proper techniques of distribution, a principle which has guided the movement since its inception: "We find that many do not make a success of the colporteur work until they have received some instruction from an experienced and successful worker. There is a particular knack required that all can possess naturally, but if not, can be acquired by intelligent perseverance."[2]

Today only the written works of Mr. Rutherford are distributed. Most Witnesses are oblivious to the fact that the founder of the movement ever wrote anything, for the Society no longer reprints or refers to the writings of Russell. Originally his works were sold only in conjunction with the Bible, but today the Witnesses seldom try to sell Bibles and apparently concentrate their efforts on dispensing Mr. Rutherford's works.

Mr. Rutherford communicated with his followers almost entirely

[1] The announced intent of the Mormons toward their secondary written sources is, I believe, essentially different.

[2] *Watch Tower,* Dec., 1892.

through his writings. Because he appeared so infrequently, the Witnesses took each new publication as his latest personal word to them as individuals. Believing these messages to be divinely inspired, they read them diligently and work strenuously to distribute millions of copies to infidels. They also believe that the writings of Mr. Rutherford are helping to bring about the end of the present age. At one meeting which I attended, the leader complained that the workers were not distributing enough books and pamphlets and warned them that they would be held responsible if Jehovah's will were thus thwarted. He explained that "mere men" could obstruct the providence of God simply by devoting too little time to the distribution of the Society's literature.

Under the compulsion of this idea, Witnesses use up most of their spare time in trudging the streets to sell the literature. Sometimes they do not care what books are bought so long as the literature is distributed. One woman, for example, kept coming to me after Watch Tower meetings to sell me one of Mr. Rutherford's books. When I asked her which book she thought I should buy, her answer was, "Buy any book; it makes no difference to me. They're all good."

On another occasion I talked with some Witnesses after we had left a meeting. They were quite angry because the central organization had introduced the latest pamphlet of Mr. Rutherford's at a meeting of another Company in the city the night before. This, they felt, was an evidence of partiality to the other Company. They themselves would be at a disadvantage if they were asked about the pamphlet and did not know of it. One bold Witness said that he would write to the Society and tell it how the group felt. New pieces of literature are never offered in large quantities; a frequent exhortation on introducing a new item is, "All should TRY to get it." Thus the acquisition of Rutherford's latest publications is made a game in which the jealousy of competing Witnesses, their eagerness to beat rivals to the goal and to increase their personal prestige, all have a part.

The literature has deep-seated significance to some Witnesses, not usually, however, to those who are busy in the propagating work, but to those who have time for careful and repeated reading. Those who study the literature often maintain a definite schedule. One Witness tells how he devotes a portion of each day for his reading: "I rise habitually at four and leave home for the shop at seven. Breakfast and other things occupy part of the time, but I get from an hour to an hour and a quarter for reading and study, and that is the best time for it." [3] This Witness tells, moreover, of his love for the Bible and of the fact that he has been able, in his early morning study periods, not only to study the works of Mr. Rutherford but also to memorize the whole Book of Isaiah. Another Witness declared after reading one of Rutherford's books, "I am satisfied that I have found the real truth, and can tell it to others." [4] Sometimes Witnesses find a book more interesting if read several times. One Witness reports: "I have read it nearly all twice over, some of it three and four times." [5]

The prolific Mr. Rutherford wrote twenty books and some five hundred articles, besides his widely distributed magazines. Rutherford claimed that he had nothing to do with the publication of his writings, but that he submitted them to the Watch Tower Bible and Tract Society. As president of the Society, however, he was in charge of the selection of all prospective publications. At the beginning of each publication a statement is made (presumably by the publisher) as to the number of copies which have thus far been printed of the particular item. Usually the first edition consists of several million copies; in the case of *Children*, published in 1941, 3,000,000 copies comprised the first printing. Sometimes mention is made of the past sales successes of Mr. Rutherford's books; for example, in the Preface to *The Crisis*, published in 1933, it is claimed that 22,213,639 copies of Mr. Rutherford's books and pamphlets were distributed during the previous year alone. The title page of *The Kingdom*, published in 1931, carries the statement: "The combined circulation of Judge Rutherford's books exceeds 93,000,000." The shortages caused by the present war have doubtless curtailed these distribution figures.

Mr. Czatt is probably correct in his opinion that this practice of emphasizing extensive distribution is simply a means of influencing new readers and of keeping old ones impressed. This seems especially true when one encounters in the *Yearbook* of the Society for 1943 a detailed list of the exact amounts of glue, paper, cloth, and so on, which were used during the previous year in the preparation of the literature.

The Society also publishes material for those to whom the regular books and pamphlets are not suited. It published literature for the blind in braille as early as 1925. A book for children, published in 1924 and called *The Way to Paradise* (the title suggests the type of religious edu-

[3] *Ibid.*, Sept., 1896.   [4] *Ibid.*, April, 1930.   [5] *Ibid.*, Jan., 1882.

cation then prevalent among the Witnesses), met with such success that a songbook was demanded as companion to the volume. The two magazines of the Society—*The Watch Tower* and *Consolation*—have, according to Witness figures, a yearly distribution of about seven million each; [6] both are biweeklies, appearing in alternate weeks. Ostensibly, anyone can contribute articles to them. A statement, now discontinued, disclosed the method by which suitable articles were chosen:

> We will inform our readers what has been our method of sifting truth that they may know of our CAREFULNESS in trying to separate truth from error.
>
> The editor seeks to test his own articles by the Word of God, but every article which appears in the paper has the special criticism of some one or more of those who are walking in the light. If it be a NEW point of interpretation, it must have the assent of at least two of those best posted and most conversant with the Scriptures before it shall appear. This rule which we apply to our own writings we apply to others also.[7]

In practice, however, there is little doubt that all the articles, regardless of authorship, were revised and approved by one person, Mr. Rutherford. Moreover, if any of them were written by anyone other than Mr. Rutherford, the fact has never been publicized. All the official publications of the Society display the same style,[8] characterized by the obvious legal phrases "to wit," "whereas," and the like. The content reveals close control over the theological concepts offered and a monotonous sameness in their explanation and presentation. The articles, moreover, have repeated the same resentments over a long period. As might be expected, there has been very little variety in literary style or ideas.

Indeed, variety of ideas was not desired by Mr. Rutherford. The Witnesses are supposed to entertain no conceptions that vary from those of their leader. If they do, they submit themselves to rigorous self-examination, because variance from the norm established by Mr. Ruther-

---

[6] *Yearbook*, 1943. *The Watch Tower* has been published since 1879; until 1916 it was edited by Russell. Originally called *Zion's Watch Tower and Herald of Christ's Presence*, it passed through several transitions until the adoption in March, 1939, of the present name, *The Watch Tower, Announcing Jehovah's Kingdom* (see the Bibliography, under Russell). *Consolation*, founded in 1916 as *The Golden Age*, received its present name in October, 1937. Since January, 1939, both have appeared in multicolored covers.

[7] *Watch Tower*, May, 1882.

[8] Some time before Rutherford's death, I had come to the conclusion that *Children*, purportedly written by him, could not have been. I reached this conclusion through certain methods of literary criticism that I applied to the movement's writings.

ford is a token of the devil's handiwork. In 1935 a full-time worker wrote to Mr. Rutherford of a struggle of this sort:

About two years ago, if I remember correctly, I wrote you a letter in which I very unwisely attempted to "interpret" some of the prophecies of God's Word. Now I see that such an effort on my part was nothing but childish prattle. I hereby offer my apology and ask your forgiveness for such presumption on my part. Jehovah has placed you in his mighty organization as the visible commander of his forces yet in the flesh. As for me, I am delighted to remain just a buck private in the ranks, and by Jehovah's grace continue to stand shoulder to shoulder with my brethren in this the greatest battle of the ages.[9]

The stifling of all religiously creative expression is one of the important traits of the movement. Few in the organization care about new ideas or methods; the Witnesses merely reproduce faithfully the words and concepts of their leader. Each week Witnesses scan the latest copy of *The Watch Tower* or *Consolation* to see what they should believe and emphasize for the week to come. A devoted believer in California writes thus of the importance of the magazines:

I would be afraid to dogmatically teach any thought that I might have if it is contrary to "The Watch Tower." The responsibility would be more than I dare assume; so I am glad to leave this responsibility with the recognized authority [Mr. Rutherford].[10]

Back copies of the magazine are available to the Witnesses, and sometime ago the Society offered a compilation of every issue of *The Watch Tower* from 1884, suitably bound for constant reference. In recent years back copies of the magazines have been sold for three cents instead of the usual five. In addition to the magazines, the Society publishes a one-page newssheet *The Kingdom News*, of which over 24,000,000 copies were distributed in 1942. Generally it contains a "lead" article and the latest happenings in the Witness work and various announcements. *The Informant*, another newssheet, is distributed only to full-time workers engaged in field service away from the central organization in Brooklyn.

Occasionally special pamphlets or posters are printed and distributed in certain localities or among certain language-speaking groups. The Society has published its literature in as many as seventy-eight languages, according to Mr. Rutherford, in an attempt to meet the needs of special

[9] *Watch Tower*, June, 1935. [10] *Ibid.*, June, 1925.

groups. Mr. Gaux, of the Brooklyn headquarters, told me of a pamphlet printed solely for distribution in a Long Island town that had passed an ordinance prohibiting the house-to-house distribution of Witness literature. Mr. Gaux explained that the circular was prepared especially to challenge the townsmen on their refusal to let the Witnesses deliver "the truth" to them. The circular was left at every door in that Long Island town one morning before dawn.

In his writings, Mr. Rutherford seldom disclaimed superior insights into either mundane or spiritual matters. Like his predecessor, he sometimes spoke directly about the sources of his ideas, but not with sufficient clarity for his followers to agree among themselves. Usually, both Russell's and Rutherford's statements on this point have been ambiguous and open to several interpretations. Russell said of one of his books that he never "considered it free from all error," yet believed that it was valuable because of "its many and fundamental truths." [11] The observer can see from this passage that in essentials Russell claimed to be preaching and writing "the truth," but admitted that in nonessentials he might sometimes be in error. Russell on one occasion openly disclaimed supernatural inspiration: "I claim nothing of superiority or supernatural power, dignity or authority, nor do I aspire to exalt myself in the estimation of my brethren." [12] Rutherford was never so moderate. Instead, he sought to imply that Jehovah was speaking through him. For example, in 1933, he said:

For more than two years it has been my privilege to address the people by radio concerning God's kingdom, which truth they so greatly need at this time. These speeches do not contain my message, but do contain the expression of Jehovah's purpose which he commands must now be told to the people.[13]

Rutherford affirmed that he was revealing God's hidden purposes to an unfriendly world; to the Witnesses this affirmation is a dogma of the faith, one of the cardinal bases of the whole Witness movement. They are perfectly sure that Jehovah spoke through Mr. Rutherford who, in turn, gave the message, through the written word, to the Witnesses.

The Witnesses, then, practically consider Rutherford's writings to be divinely inspired. So conceived, the books often exert a profound influence upon the individual reader. A Witness writes of one of them:

[11] *Ibid.*, May, 1882.   [12] *Ibid.*, July, 1906.
[13] Rutherford, *Why Serve Jehovah?* p. 62.

I find myself thirsting for more knowledge from this seemingly inspired pen. Permit me to say that I have never read or heard anything equal to that little volume in its influence upon my heart and life; to my mind it answers most grandly and conclusively the great question: "Is life worth living?" Such views as it sets forth are bound to find responses in the minds and hearts of all unbiased, thinking Christians, for they bear the stamp of something greater than mere human conception.[14]

Those who doubt the divine origin of Rutherford's writings, who cede that Rutherford is merely a man speaking his own opinion, are sometimes accused of "playing with the Devil."

The belief in the sacred nature of the Society's publications is as old as the Society itself. In an early issue of *The Watch Tower*, a reader wrote to Russell: "Was this book a REVELATION? Where did you get those clear ideas? They must have come from above, for all wisdom comes from God."[15] When Mr. Rutherford published his book, *Light*, a Witness wrote to him:

The conviction is pressed upon me deeply now that no human creature is the author of LIGHT. No man could write that book. No man wrote LIGHT. It is the manifest power of a living God that gave to us the wonderful revelation of his Word of Truth.[16]

In the same year another wrote: "Brother, you were merely the amanuensis in the production of LIGHT. Jehovah is its author, even as the book itself declares."[17]

Many of the Witnesses believe that Mr. Rutherford was given special insight into biblical interpretations that are of import to our age. They feel that certain parts of the Bible apply only to particular periods in human history, and that a passage of Scripture which applies to one period cannot be understood by persons living in another. To illustrate: One of the leaders of the Harlem Company in New York City told me that the group planned to study the eleventh and twelfth chapters of the Book of Daniel in their monthly meetings. He said that this book, and particularly those chapters, had always bewildered readers because the content did not seem to fit into any historical scheme. This Witness told me that the true meaning of the whole book had been revealed to Mr. Rutherford who was making its meaning clear through the maga-

---

[14] *Watch Tower*, Dec., 1881.
[15] *Ibid.*, May, 1882.
[16] *Ibid.*, April, 1931.
[17] *Ibid.*

zines. When I asked him why the book was not clear hitherto, he said that God had not chosen to make it so.

Because the literature is considered divinely inspired, the means by which it reaches a new convert sometimes seem to be an act of God. One Witness related to me that he first discovered the books of Mr. Rutherford in an empty house in which he was working. He said that he had opened a closet door and found a number of Witness papers and books. During his lunch hour, he began to read what he had found. That afternoon he was troubled by what he had read and finally came to the conclusion that God had willed that he open the closet door and read the literature. Today he proudly tells this story as positive proof that God is so intimately connected with the literature that he is aiding in its distribution by what "men call accidental ways." [18]

In his later years, Mr. Rutherford wrote no predictions to bolster the zeal of his flock. This may mean that he learned well from the experiences of Mr. Russell, whose imprecision as a prophet was his undoing. Russell's religion, derived in part from the Second Adventists, was indissolubly linked with the idea of "the future hope." To him the doctrine of the second coming of Jesus was most important. Many of Russell's followers lived for the day when they should witness the destruction which was to be followed by a paradise for true believers. Mr. Russell's predictions sometimes took this form: in twenty-six years (from 1889) the "present governments will be overthrown and dissolved." [19] At other times, however, he would foretell a Wellsian Utopia. While in these more optimistic moods he would prove how increasing socialization of property and community conveniences would issue in a rather sublime, ease-granting society. But when the sober realization of the deep-seated sinfulness of men was dominant, this gold-at-the-end-of-the-rainbow society would vanish from his writings. Even his most cherished concession to worldliness, namely, socialism, would disappear:

We have reason to believe that Socialism will make great progress in the next ten years. But frequently it will not be wisely or moderately advanced . . . and as a result, impatience will lead to calamity.[20]

When Mr. Rutherford assumed the leadership of the organization, he faithfully expressed the mind-set of those whom Russell had helped

[18] A similar case is recorded in *The Watch Tower*, Oct., 1885.
[19] Russell, *Studies in the Scriptures*, II, 98–99.   [20] *Ibid.*, IV, 485–486.

along for years with the hope of a perfectly ordered society. In 1921 Rutherford predicted that the end of the then-existing social order would occur within the lifetime of that generation. What he meant precisely by this observation is difficult to perceive, but the statement seemed quite clear to his followers, who immediately were driven to more intensive proselyting activity and to last-minute preparation for the coming catastrophe. The Booklet, *Millions Now Living Will Never Die,* which announced Rutherford's prediction, was distributed as extensively as any of his other writings have ever been. The theme of the booklet was so rich an energizer of his followers and so compelling an idea in itself that even as late as 1932 Mr. Rutherford was still delivering talks upon it. In that year he declared that the religious work of the Witnesses was "coming to a conclusion," that the end was "only a short time away," and that the end was "much less than the length of a generation."

Unlike Mr. Russell, Rutherford seemingly was not interested in any "worldly" panacea for the period of evil which was to precede the golden age; but then, from the movement's history he had learned much about the appeals to which people respond. Indeed, he seems to have learned so much that, in his later years, he was unwilling to prophesy at all.

Rutherford used the Bible as absolute proof of the accuracy of his views. To him, merely to quote a verse of the Bible which even remotely had some bearing upon the subject was to end a debate victoriously. Any verse from the Bible was as authoritative as any other. There was no consideration for the period in which it was written, for its background or historical meaning. The Witnesses do not consider the Bible as a complex, human document with a legion of contributors, expressing various stages of religious development, and written under widely varying social conditions:

Thus do we find: one plan, spirit, aim, and purpose pervades the entire book. Its opening pages record the creation and fall of man; its closing pages tell of man's recovery from that fall; and its intervening pages show the successive steps of the plan of God for the accomplishment of this purpose.[21]

When the Witnesses are asked about the trustworthiness of the Bible, they often answer in the words of their founder: "There is a straight-forwardness about the Bible that stamps it as the truth." [22] Many of the

[21] *Ibid.,* I, 56.   [22] *Ibid.,* 41.

full-time workers are imbued thoroughly with love for the Bible, making it their constant source of fortification against the rebuffs they encounter in their field work. Once in a meeting the leader asked the audience how many knew from memory a certain verse in the Book of Matthew. Nearly half of the Witnesses had memorized the verse. On another occasion, upon the sentencing of eleven Witnesses to ten days in jail, I saw an excited Witness jump to his feet in the courtroom and with open Bible read the tenth verse of the second chapter of the Book of Revelation: "Have no fear of what you are to suffer. The devil indeed is going to put some of you in prison, that you may be tested; you will have a distressful ten days! Be faithful."

Opposing what it calls "modern criticism of the Bible," yet making use of a few of the methods of biblical interpretation developed in recent years, the movement generally has succeeded in endearing the Bible to its followers.[23] Witnesses relate that their interest in the writings of Mr. Rutherford has enriched their appreciation of it: "My Bible is no longer a book of a dead language; it is a mine of wealth." [24] Again, a woman Witness writes: "Only last night my husband said, 'Well, if I did not know we had the same old family Bible, I should have thought that we had a different translation.' " [25]

The extent to which the Jehovah's Witnesses has been successful is in no small part due to the veneration in which the Bible is commonly held among the masses. The Witnesses believe that their particular interpretation is correct, and that without the Bible nothing of what they say could be true. This attitude is strikingly evident when they approach persons who do not "believe in the Bible" as "the infallible guide for faith and practice." In such cases the Witnesses usually cannot bridge the gap between belief in the Bible as they conceive it and other evaluations of the book. A few Witnesses tell me that they do not attempt to convert anyone who does not first believe in God and the Bible.

For many years the Society has believed that door-to-door canvassing has succeeded not only in distributing the literature most efficiently, but also in attracting the greatest number of new converts. At first, the Witnesses carried their literature in brief cases, but the task of bearing a large number of books and pamphlets was burdensome, especially for women and children. As early as 1908, the Society sought a remedy in the invention and sale of the "Dawn-mobile," a wheeled contraption

[23] *Ibid.*, II, 55; I, 43.   [24] *Watch Tower*, May, 1881.   [25] *Ibid.*, March, 1883.

that could be fitted on any suitcase. The worker was relieved of carrying his load which he now simply pushed along the street like a baby carriage. Years after this means seemed outmoded, Mr. Rutherford employed the technique of speaking to countless thousands on the radio each week. For ten years he spoke regularly over some two hundred radio stations. Because of the controversial nature of his talks, however, many of the stations banned the program, an action that was charged against the Roman Catholic Hierarchy. Ultimately, the radio technique, like the Dawn-mobiles, was found to be disadvantageous.

In 1937 the Society introduced portable phonographs for the use of full-time workers (and any others who could afford them). By 1942, the Society reported that it had placed over 35,000 of these phonographs in the hands of Witnesses and that it was distributing about 300,000 records each year. The phonographs were manufactured at the Brooklyn factory and sold for ten dollars. Mr. Rutherford made a series of recordings, of which the first impressions were made by a commercial house in the East while mass production was carried on by a firm in Hollywood, California. By 1939, Rutherford had made over 109 different recordings, some of which were transcribed into various foreign languages. Use of the phonograph gave the Witnesses greater confidence in their house-to-house canvassing—the message was spoken for them. As one Witness testified: "Now the ice is broken with the glorious talking machine. One has such a feeling of security when one uses it as occasion presents itself." [26] In 1942, recordings were thus played more than ten million times.

The phonograph was later improved by the invention of a worker at the factory in Brooklyn. This improved phonograph saves setting the "arm" for production, shuts off automatically, and can be played lying on its side. Within the latest model is a compartment large enough to hold several sandwiches and several of Mr. Rutherford's books. Thousands of these gray-colored phonographs have been bought by the Witnesses who wish to be "up to the minute" in their field-work techniques.

The Society also owns "sound cars" which are automobiles, usually trucks, rigged up with amplifying systems of sufficient volume to reach large audiences. In 1941, the Society announced that about 323 of these units were being used in this country. They are operated sometimes in rural areas where they can traverse sparsely settled roads and bring the Witness message to farmers. More often they are used in small towns on

[26] *Ibid.*, March, 1938.

Saturday nights, when they are placed at prominent intersections. At the time of the international conventions the sound cars are ordered to the area of the convention to ease the work of the door-to-door canvassers.

The operators of the sound trucks, as well as all other full-time workers, constitute a special group within the organization of the Jehovah's Witnesses. Although the present-day Witnesses claim to have no elite within their ranks who might be termed a "priesthood," nevertheless, upon close observation this appears to be a self-deception. No stronger hatred do the Witnesses feel than that for "the clergy-class," who, according to the standard Witness interpretation, simply use religion as a means of maintaining their social position and of controlling the common people for "the commercial and political interests." Witnesses are united in the belief that a religious movement which has a clergy is ruled by the Devil. And yet, if the facts are faced fairly, the truth seems to be that even the Jehovah's Witnesses has been unable to manage its complex, scattered organization without the aid of special elites.

The Society, moreover, has not always felt that such a group was detrimental to its purposes. As early as 1894 Mr. Russell gave to full-time workers "Letters of Introduction" authorizing them "to take a leading part in gatherings," to serve the Holy Sacrament (or the "Memorial Supper," as it was known among Witnesses), and to perform other functions normally fulfilled by the clergy of other religious groups. These "Letters of Introduction" were valid for one year and were renewable. In them Mr. Russell endorsed the moral character of the bearer and his zeal and understanding of the Bible, but carefully refrained from any statement as to his educational qualifications for these priestly tasks. In fact, no college or seminary training was required; the distinction between such workers and priests had to be made clear because of the Society's antipathy toward the latter as a class. Even so, the Witnesses objected strongly to those who came among them seeking to run their affairs and, finally, after much discontent, the "Letters of Introduction" were discontinued.[27]

A further stratification of the workers is evident from the existence, up to the time of Russell's death, of two groups of elected officers in every local company: the elders and the deacons. Elders were entrusted with final authority in the Company, although their actual function was supposed to be "spiritual" only. Deacons were in charge of the more

[27] *Ibid.*, Oct., 1894.

mundane affairs of the organization. They arranged for the paying of rent, the announcements of meetings, the distribution of the literature, and so on. As the organization became larger, elders were usually full-time workers sent by the central organization to a specific area of work, similarly to the service directors of today. During this later period the elders represented the central organization, while the deacons were home-town people who did the bulk of the real work.

Aside from this actual differentiation in terms of function, a more theoretical classification separated the believers, during the lifetime of Mr. Russell. Frequently Russell spoke of "a Sanctuary Class" and of members of "the Seed of Promise," as though these Witnesses were distinct from the ordinary run of believer. The members of these divisions "felt themselves to be sure of their calling of God." In this sense, consequently, the early Witnesses were divided into those who believed but were not sure of their "election," and those who believed and also felt certain that they were "called of God." [28] This theoretical division led to sharp differences in later years over eligibility for the Memorial Supper and has resulted in a distinction between believers which exists even to this day.[29]

In his later life, Russell was prone to group all believers into four separate "classes." First, there were those who knew that they were true believers and, being "dead with Christ," were fulfilling their "covenant." Second, there were those, a larger group, who were "spirit-begotten" and "covenanted," but who "did nothing about it." Third, there were those who were "justified, but not sanctified." Finally, there were "wolves in sheep's clothing," who were hypocritical in religious duties.[30] Russell believed that it was almost impossible to recognize another person as a member of one of these four groups, but that it should not be difficult for the individual believer himself to know in which group he fell.

Within recent years the movement has developed a wider system of classification, which is, of course, a "religious" one. Present-day Witnesses think of people as divided into four groups. The first includes the "goats"—"all those who ill-treat the persons who are devoted to God and his kingdom"; [31] in its broader meaning this group is composed of

[28] Russell, *Studies in the Scriptures*, III, 188.

[29] Rutherford, *Jehovah's Organization*, p. 14.

[30] Russell, *Studies in the Scriptures*, I, 235–238.

[31] Rutherford, *Armageddon*, p. 58.

those who have heard "the truth" as preached by the Witnesses and have definitely refused to believe. The second group, called "other sheep," are those who never have had the chance of deciding for themselves whether they would accept the Witness message. The third is composed of all who are "saved" but do not have any special "sign" from Jehovah of their redemption. These are called "Jonadabs," after the Old Testament character of that name who renounced Baalism in favor of Jahwehism.[32] The fourth group are those true believers who by a kind of mystical experience know that they are of the 144,000 faithful (mentioned in the Book of Revelation) comprising the special "body" of Jehovah. I have met such Witnesses. Of the classifications propounded at various times by the Society's leaders, I have found this recent one to be the most prevalent. Witnesses are vitally interested in classifying those whom they meet as to their placement in this scheme.

Although the foregoing discussion is directed toward discovering whether the Jehovah's Witnesses has a "clergy class," it can only suggest several lines of division, sometimes of a most theoretical nature. Actually, the local organization of the Company in terms of appointed and elected officers seems to be sufficient evidence of at least a form of "clergy." Further evidence is found in the presence of two orders among the Witnesses. Certain Witnesses are classified by the local Company (a duplicate record is also kept by the central organization) either as "Publishers" or as "Pioneers." A Publisher is a part-time worker; a Pioneer, a full-time worker. It is proper to become a Publisher before becoming a Pioneer, although there is no strict rule about the matter. The Publisher may work as much as he cares, and often, like Thornton Wilder's George Brush, he proselytes as he goes about his regular employment. Commonly, however, the Publisher pledges a certain minimum number of hours per month to the local service director. In one Company which I visited the minimum for a Publisher was thirty hours a month, although the Society expects a minimum of sixty hours. In periods when the organization is making a special drive for converts and for the distribution of literature, the minimum number of hours is increased. In 1943, among Witnesses throughout the world there were 106,000 Publishers, 64,995 of them in the United States; the corresponding figures for the Pioneers were 7,624 and 4,204.

The name "Pioneer" was first introduced in 1934; in the earliest years

[32] Rutherford, *Angels*, p. 63. See also p. 115, below.

full-time workers were called "Pilgrims" and later, "Heralds." Mr. Russell mentioned the first full-time worker as a Mr. J. B. Adamson who left "a profitable business paying about $1,500 a year as well as other things." [33] About the time that Adamson became a full-time worker, Robert Bailey and J. C. Sunderlin also gave up their regular employment to become field representatives of Mr. Russell. In the early days the Society compiled annual itineraries for these full-time workers, and their food and lodging were supplied by faithful Witnesses along the way.

The Pioneers are the backbone of the Witness organization, for it is chiefly they who go about from town to town distributing the literature and seeking converts. They are, as a group, thoroughly consecrated to the program and eager to sacrifice everything, if necessary, for the work to which they believe Jehovah has called them. The degree of their fidelity and perseverance is illustrated in the story of a physician who was called in to administer to a sick Pioneer. The doctor said that the man seemed "young, active, and to all appearances healthy and vigorous" but upon examination he was found to be "just on the verge of a nervous breakdown." [34] In the doctor's opinion this condition was brought on by excessive physical strain. The young man's behavior is a type admired by some Witnesses, who would place his zeal high in their scale of values. Indeed, many try to emulate such examples. [35]

Pioneers do not allow family difficulties to interfere with their work. In the following report, a traveling Pioneer writes of his method of solving such a dilemma:

While I was colporteuring in Tennessee last spring and just making expenses, the mail one day brought a letter revealing such stringent conditions at home that it looked as though there was but one thing for me to do: Abandon the service and resume secular employment, at least until the emergency was over. Some affected by this experience read it as the Lord's leadings that I should leave the work. But Brother F—— and I decided that we would try to stay in the colporteur service and also to meet the obligations which had arisen.

The letter had come on Friday. We had fully made up our minds early Saturday, and Monday we sold practically twice as many books as we had ever done before, and continued to do so until we left Tennessee for the Convention, having met without strain the exigency.

[33] *Watch Tower*, June, 1881.　　[34] *Ibid.*, Dec., 1920.　　[35] *Ibid.*, March, 1922.

The very next "Bulletin" bore out the fact that some of the Lord's people are prone to interpret the tests which overtake them while in the Lord's work, as divine leadings that they should leave the work; while in reality the Lord is simply testing them to see if their determination to stay in the work is still what it should be.[36]

Most of the Pioneers travel about the country working in assigned areas at the direction of the central organization. A worker may be ordered from one locale to another without any reason being given. One Pioneer told me that she had received a letter from the Society telling her to pack up and be ready to move as soon as she received a second letter announcing her destination—a case of marching under sealed orders! Nevertheless the job appeals to many young people, girls as well as men, who are looking for travel, adventure, and increased participation in the Witness program of world redemption. Pioneers are given room, board, clothing, minimal traveling expenses, and ten dollars a month as an allowance—the same as any full-time worker either in the Brooklyn factory or on the farms. Missionaries sent abroad by the Society work on the same basis as do the Pioneers at home. Mr. Rutherford, as some Witnesses are proud to recall, was a Pioneer before he became attached to the legal department of the Society, and in a sense was still a Pioneer while president of the Board.

Pioneers located in large cities often specialize in a particular kind of "witnessing." Some are assigned to apartment dwellings, others to stores, still others to business houses. The Witnesses use different techniques in approaching their specialized tasks. One Pioneer complained to the Society that he was refused a phonograph because "being in the special business-house service I am unable to use the phonograph as much as those who are in the ordinary service." [37] Most of the special Pioneers with whom I have talked said that they would "do nothing else," and each thought his special function to be the most valuable to the Society and satisfying to himself.

In the performance of their chosen duty both Pioneers and Publishers work with a zeal which only religious motivation can provide. The Witnesses are not apologetic in their approach to unbelievers, but, rather, paraphrasing the words of the Psalmist, they "glow like a bridegroom leaving his chamber, exult like a hero to run his course," and in the execution of their mission nothing escapes their ardor.

[36] *Ibid.*, Oct., 1924.   [37] *Ibid.*, May, 1938.

When I first began to study the Jehovah's Witnesses, I was fortunate enough to secure the fine help of one of the counsels of the American Civil Liberties Union. In introducing me to the investigation he said, in effect:

Probably you have never seen anyone who is willing actually to die for his religious convictions. With our sophisticated ways of doing things, and with our mentalities which seem never to deal with absolute certainties, we moderns think that there is nothing for which a man should give his life. But when you meet the Witnesses, you will be meeting, probably for the first time, people who are willing to be persecuted, even slain, for the sake of their religious faith.

At the time I was not entirely convinced. Now I am. I am confident that the Witnesses demonstrate one of the most sacrificial ways of living which has been seen in many decades. So profound is the sincerity of faith of the Witnesses that even the impartial observer Mr. Czatt says: "There are some beautiful Christian characters among them." [38] They are willing to give up friends and family, to work indefatigably in their spare hours, to give unstintingly of their money, to withstand bitter persecution, and even, in certain European countries, to remain loyal to their convictions unto death—all for "the cause." Mr. Rutherford, in speaking of the persecution which the Witnesses have undergone in Germany alone, said, shortly before his death, that probably there were about 6,000 Witnesses in prison camps, and of these "many have been shot." [39] In most of the United Nations at the present time—with the notable exceptions of England and the United States—the movement is banned.

The Witnesses on the whole believe that the fundamental task which confronts them in these confused and tragic times is the spreading of their message. One Company in Texas sent this report to the Society: "Believing the service in the form of witnessing from door to door is the paramount duty of the followers of Christ today, this Company has striven to faithfully perform such work in this locality." [40] Few members of any religious denomination are working for their ends as energetically as are most of the Witnesses. Even the children are encouraged to engage in door-to-door canvassing as soon as they are old enough to do so. From California a Publisher writes:

[38] Milton Stacey Czatt, *The International Bible Students*, p. 22.
[39] Rutherford, *Judge Rutherford Uncovers the Fifth Column*, p. 20.
[40] *Watch Tower*, Sept., 1934.

My boy eleven years old has learned his canvass; he has already disposed of about eighty books. Many people are impressed with these children when they knock at the doors and offer a religious book. My little girl, eight years old, canvasses whenever she can, and has disposed of a number of books. One lady was glad to purchase six books from her.[41]

In the spread of their message the Witnesses have pledged their determination to "keep on keeping on" until "our course is finished in death." [42] Sometimes in attempting to convince people of "the truth" they find it necessary to resort to subterfuge, but this does not disturb them because they feel that whatever they do is for the glory of Jehovah and his coming kingdom:

I have been able to get several Catholics to take "The Kingdom News" by telling them: "It is a little newspaper. Surely your priests don't keep you from reading the newspapers." Their usual reply: "O, no, they will let us read that." [43]

Many Witnesses report that they find Roman Catholic people more difficult to convert than Protestants and infidels, although some Witnesses feel that Roman Catholics are the most "gullible." Generally, however, the Witnesses do not give so much attention to the conversion of Catholics as they give to that of others. Sometimes Witnesses assemble in front of churches on Sunday mornings to distribute their literature; seldom do they include Roman Catholic churches; in the words of one Witness, "We exclude Roman Catholics from the volunteer service because the vast majority of their attendants are either too ignorant or too bigoted to read and think for themselves." [44]

In the promulgation of their truth the Witnesses often meet violent opposition. Sometimes their cars are burned, their literature is destroyed, their property invaded, and they themselves are maligned and beaten. The report of the American Civil Liberties Union says of them:

Not since the persecution of the Mormons years ago has any religious minority been so bitterly and generally attacked as the members of Jehovah's Witnesses—particularly in the spring and summer of 1940. While this was the peak of the attacks upon them, hostility and discrimination have been rife for several years.[45]

But this persecution, bitter as it is, does not deflect the Witnesses from their course. The intense physical and mental suffering which they some-

[41] *Ibid.*, Feb., 1927.   [42] *Watch Tower*, March, 1924.
[43] *Ibid.*, Jan., 1940.   [44] *Ibid.*, April, 1900.
[45] American Civil Liberties Union, *The Persecution of the Jehovah's Witnesses*, p. 1.

times undergo is compensated for by the belief that persecution is one of the earmarks of the end of the age: "The more opposition and persecution from Satan's organization we endure, the nearer we know we are to his final destruction and to the vindication of Jehovah's name." [46] This almost masochistic tendency in the Witnesses brings great satisfaction to those who can endure.

The Witnesses often speak in their meetings of the persecutions they have undergone. Men workers tell of being thrust bodily from apartment buildings; women workers who go from door-to-door tell of the abuse to which they are subjected. After such recitals are finished, all seek comfort from the books of Mr. Rutherford and from the Bible. I have attended a house meeting at which Witnesses told each other of their humiliating experiences in the field. Following the confessions, the leader dimmed the lights and all sat about the room with fixed faces glowing in the dull light, listening to the words of Psalm 46:

> God is a shelter and stronghold for us,
>   we shall find him very near;
>   therefore we never fear,
> Though earth be overset,
>   and the hills sink deep in the sea.
> Let billows roar and foam,
>   let mountains shake under the storm;
>   the Lord of Hosts is at our side,
>   the God of Jacob is our fortress.[47]

After the leader finished, some Witnesses dried wet cheeks, some heaved long sighs, others gritted their teeth; all were refreshed.

Of course the Witnesses are not always persecuted in their field work. Many times they find people receptive and willing to listen. The degree of persecution which they have withstood should not dwarf the high degree of success which also they have achieved. Contrary to the common opinion of the Witnesses, not all policemen put them in jail:

Sunday we used the phonograph in the home of the chief of police. They were highly pleased with the records. They had some of the books and took more. The chief was so delighted with the lectures that he extended a cordial invitation to call again.[48]

Sometimes when their efforts do not bring the desired results, the Witnesses believe that they are not sufficiently consecrated, and they

[46] *Watch Tower*, June, 1935.   [48] *Watch Tower*, March, 1935.
[47] James Moffatt, *The Bible: a New Translation* (New York, Harper and Bros., 1926).

pray, therefore, for greater faith. One Witness, a veteran of field work, says: "I think sometimes it is because I am so unworthy that the Lord don't use me more." [49] Other times, when they become discouraged they put the blame elsewhere:

This week I canvassed two homes: one large and fine, the other small and poor. A man answered the bell at the first. I told him that I called to show him a Home Bible Study Course which the International Bible Students' Association were putting out. He had reached for the book, but the minute he heard "International Bible Students' Association" he stepped back into the house saying, "The International Bible Students' Association? No! No! No!" [50]

The man who closed the door had been instructed by his local minister not to buy anything from members of that Association. The Witness in this case felt that the blame for the man's refusal rested upon the invidious minister who, as a member of "the clergy-class," desired the destruction of the Jehovah's Witnesses.

The joys of participating in field work very largely compensate for all these rebuffs. One young Spanish-speaking Witness told me that he could hardly wait for the opportunity to "witness" to others because he said he "always feels so good after witnessing." He further told me that he was thrilled to find a family, especially one of many members, who would ask him in to discuss the intricacies of the Witness theology. Similar joys are expressed by a female Witness:

I am going out in the work rain or shine. I cannot stay out of it when we see such wonderful opportunities. . . . Why I find no one who does not want to hear all about this wonderful message, and all agree more or less that it must be true. Some days I have sold thirty-five to thirty-eight books. [51]

Some Witnesses are roused to accelerated participation in field work by intimate, sentimental stories which they seek to match in their own experiences. These "success stories" circulate and expand, like oft-told tales, among the members of local Companies. The following is an example:

One day while calling at my first house I met at the door a sweet little mother and two children. I canvassed them for the complete set. The little girl of ten said: "O, mother, take them! I will give you $1.00; let's buy them; we will know more than our preacher!" I sold her twenty-three books. [52]

[49] *Ibid.*, April, 1897.   [50] *Ibid.*, Sept., 1924.   [51] *Ibid.*, July, 1924.   [52] *Ibid.*

Mr. Rutherford, moreover, provided many Witnesses with an example which they might emulate:

Brother Rutherford, I would like to say for your own encouragement, that your absolute fearlessness, confidence in God, and patient endurance of afflictions have greatly strengthened many of the Lord's dear people.[53]

(Most of the qualities of Mr. Rutherford which Witnesses seek to imitate they can have learned about only through his writings.) Thus strengthened for the most part with compensatory experiences the Witnesses continue in great cheer to "preach the word in season and out of season." Not many find the course too arduous. For a Witness to have been in the movement for ten or twenty years is not exceptional, and some have been with the organization for even longer periods:

I am seventy-nine years old. Have been in the service for thirty-three years. Each day has been happier than the last since I have seen the Father's wonderful purposes. The glorious prospect transports me, and the precious promises fill me with peace that passeth all understanding. My life is filled with praise.[54]

The Publishers and Pioneers who distribute the Society's literature, being not only unordained ministers, but also door-to-door peddlers, have been arrested on various charges directed toward curbing their preaching. Each Publisher and Pioneer is supplied with a card indicating his official capacity and connection with the Society. These cards, carried by the Witnesses at all times, are presented to any policeman who arrests them.

Most of the strife which their preaching brought the Witnesses was mitigated when the United States Supreme Court ruled in the case of *Lovell* vs. *City of Griffin* that Witnesses are within their rights in visiting people's homes and distributing religious literature without a license. Local ordinances which required a license for the sale of printed matter containing religious information or opinion were declared invalid. On the surface, the decisions of various courts which have upheld the Witnesses' constitutional rights have been encouraging to the Witnesses themselves and to Americans seeking to be faithful to the Bill of Rights. There can be found in some of the so-called "liberal" court decisions, however, a definition of the limits to which the courts will tolerate freedom of speech. Thus, in a case in New Haven, Connecticut, in which

[53] *Ibid.*, May, 1921.　　　　[54] *Ibid.*, April, 1934.

three Witnesses were charged "with holding people up to contempt because of their creed or religion," the Common Pleas Court judge declared just how much freedom the courts would allow the Witnesses:

I regard them [the books circulated by the three Witnesses] as matters which the author may lawfully write and the accused lawfully possess. . . . I am as little willing to declare them unlawful per se as I would be to declare that a Christian may not argue the Divinity of Christ, a Jew deny it, and a Confucianist ignore it as a legend. It is not the function of the courts to either coerce or curb thinking or expression, but at most to restrain LICENSE of expression as related to the time, place and circumstances, all of which must be related in the final analysis to the question of potential danger to the established order as represented by the system of government accepted by the people as a whole.[55]

In this decision one can see the conservative character of the courts, which the Witnesses claim are so largely bound up with "the established order." It is against "the established order" in religion and in government that the Witnesses direct their accusations. If this movement ever seriously threatened the status quo, what the courts and government would do is foreknown.

Territory No. ....

PUBLISHER'S FIELD SERVICE REPORT

To be turned in at the next company meeting following this activity.

Name .... **Address** ....

(Write plainly)

City or Town .... **State** ....

Daily Report for ....

(Month)   (Day)   (Year)

(Report below your field-service activities for the ENTIRE DAY.)

Total Books	Total Booklets	Hours of Field Service	New WT. and Consolation Subs	Individual Magazines	Sound Attendance	Back-Calls

QUOTA: 60 hours, 12 back-calls, and one book study can be attained by diligence and regularity in the service.

Remarks:

---

[55] *Liberty to Preach*, pp. 9–10.

As the Witnesses go about their canvassing, they keep records of their activities. In the central offices master records are compiled from these day-by-day reports. After a day's work the Witnesses make out a "Field Service Report" (see page 68).

Special forms are supplied to each worker for magazine subscriptions secured in the service work. These slips are kept by the central organization and probably form the only membership list of the Witnesses. Such a list, however, would probably include some non-Witnesses who are sympathetic or interested enough to subscribe to the magazines. The Society has never admitted the existence of such a list. The subscription form for *The Watch Tower* follows:

NAME ....

(Typewrite or print plainly)

STREET and NUMBER ....

CITY .... STATE ....

☐ NEW   Enter the above name as a subscriber for ⎰ 1 year ☐
☐ RENEWAL   *The Watchtower* for (check √) ⎱ 6 months ☐

Sent in by ....

THE WATCH TOWER
    117 ADAMS ST., BROOKLYN, N. Y.

Please √ Pioneer .... Company publisher ....
Send original *only* to this office. Subscriber should KEEP duplicate as receipt. Subscriber's own initials, verifying this slip as correct (   )

The Witnesses, having called at a home once, are willing to keep coming back until the occupants have accepted or rejected "the truth." Not only do the Witnesses keep records of the homes to which they pay initial visits, but they also have "back-call" slips which are intended both for their own reference and for the local service director's records. A copy of a "back-call" report appears on page 70.

The reverse side of the slip is arranged for twenty-four additional back-calls and for listing the number of phonograph records played each time. Sometimes even twenty-four back-calls are not sufficient to elicit a direct "Yes" or "No" answer; the slip is retained until the caller decides that the contact is "dead," and is then turned in to the local service director. Each time a back-call is made, a "Back-Call Follow-Up Report" is also turned in. At the present time the Society claims that approximately 7,000,000 back-calls are made annually.

Back-Call

Held at _____ Terr. No. _____
                              Name

Address _____

Date _____ Language (or Colored) _____

What day and time is most
    convenient for back-call? _____

What literature does person have? _____

Subscriber for *Watchtower?* [ ] *Consolation?* [ ]

Remarks: _____

_____

_____

Name of publisher making first call'

The reverse of the back-call slip is as follows:

DATE OF LATEST CALL	RECORDS RUN OR STUDY CONDUCTED	DATE OF LATEST CALL	RECORDS RUN OR STUDY CONDUCTED

Each time publisher makes a back-call, a Back-Call Follow-Up Report should be turned in.

A full report on the canvassing activities is usually given by the individual Witnesses at the end of each month. The data obtained from the foregoing types of reports are kept diligently by the service director and are computed both for the Company's wall chart and for the central organization.

Back-Call Follow-Up Report

(To be turned in after each back-call whether the name is in the permanent back-call file or not)

Name _____ Terr. No. _____

Address _____

Date back-call made .... Literature placed ....

( ) Back-Call   Records Run (List numbers): ....
( ) Model Study   } (Check which)
( ) Back-Call Book Study }   Publication studied: ....

Has this person attended a company book study, a "Watchtower" study, or a service meeting? _____
If person not interested, check here ( ) and attach original Back-Call slip.

_____
Name of publisher making call
(Total number of back-calls should also be reported on Publisher's Field Service Report)

8-3

The Converts and Conversion

To DISCOVER ACCURATELY the social status of the Witnesses is a task still to be accomplished. So closely have the Witnesses guarded their movement from outsiders that it is at present impossible to obtain any kind of information about them which would profitably respond to statistical methods. Outsiders have tried to gather detailed information about the members, but so far they have not succeeded very well. The Witnesses themselves are not interested in aiding a scientific survey.

When I first began my research, I devised a set of questions on the social status and other aspects of the Jehovah's Witnesses for use in interviewing. But I soon found that they withdrew their confidence from me whenever I attempted any formal interrogation. Many objected to a scientific study of their cult because they feared that I might use the information to hurt their interests as Witnesses; they were sure that the Society opposed all such investigations; they had no concern in giving any time to me except to help me find "the truth," if I were sincerely seeking it; they felt that the data I was collecting were too trivial. One Witness told me when I approached him for some information: "You might as well save your shoe leather; we do not know anything which is not in the Judge's books." Another Witness, a Pioneer, insisted that there was little to be gained from a study of the various aspects of the movement's beliefs because "all of the Witnesses think alike."

My experience is confirmed by the reports of other investigators. Mr. Czatt, who tried in the early thirties to get definite information about the social status of the Witnesses, tells that he sent out 500 copies of a questionnaire to ministers and laymen (not Witnesses) in the United States, Canada, and Hawaii, "in an attempt to obtain accurate information concerning the numerical strength, education, economic and social standing, political loyalty, and fundamental interests of the Bible Students." From the returns, he deduced that:

the Bible Students are reluctant to talk about factual matters pertaining to their organization. A copy of the questionnaire which came to the attention of Judge Rutherford called forth a protest in "The Golden Age" for March 6th, 1929, under the title "The Timely Warning." He [Rutherford] denounced the writer [Czatt] as being "employed by the active members of Satan's organization to gather information," and advised the readers of "The Golden Age" to have nothing to do with him.[1]

[1] Milton Stacey Czatt, *The International Bible Students,* pp. 20–21.

Finding that upon such returns as he got he could not construct a consistent, detailed description of the Jehovah's Witnesses, Czatt then tried to contact Witnesses directly. He addressed fifty letters to active Witnesses, asking them various questions of fact. Eleven of the fifty made replies which "contained little." The uncommunicativeness of these Witnesses, Czatt found, "accurately reflected the central authority of the movement." [2]

Mr. Czatt writes in his dissertation that he discovered few Witnesses with college degrees. Although some are professional men, most have "very limited education." He unearthed little worthy of mention about the economic level of the Witnesses, but got the "impression" that they are "predominantly laborers, mechanics, factory-workers, and farmers, with an occasional mention of semi-skilled or skilled workers." He came upon a few "retired farmers" or "older retired people" in the movement.[3]

Czatt's is one of the finest studies of the Witnesses yet made, and his vague conclusions on the social status of the Witnesses should not detract from its general value. His investigation is vastly superior to those which have appeared in popular magazines. Mr. Charles R. Walker published in *McCall's* of November, 1940, an article, "Fifth Column Jitters," in which he charges that "most of the 'Witnesses' are of German blood." Such statements are simply not true. They wrong the Witnesses and make much more difficult the task of gathering material about them.

The first impediment to a scientific study was the uncoöperativeness of the leader. Under the guise of protecting the movement from its enemies, Mr. Rutherford succeeded for years in concealing the facts about his organization. He denounced all articles written by outsiders as false and detrimental "to the true interests of Jehovah's kingdom." On the few occasions when he answered inquiries, he charged that the meaning of his statements was invariably distorted. In 1940 Mr. Logan of the New York *Evening Post* sought to obtain from Mr. Rutherford definite, first-hand information for a series of articles that Logan was writing for his paper. The interview was refused. But Logan was told that he could submit a series of questions and, if the questions were proper or interesting enough, Mr. Rutherford would probably answer them. In this par-

[2] *Ibid.*   [3] *Ibid.*, p. 21.

ticular case Mr. Rutherford did reply, although, as already noted, evasively. First Mr. Rutherford, and later the Witnesses, denounced what Logan wrote as distortions of "the facts."

In a booklet (*The Theocracy*) published a year later, Mr. Rutherford described the incident thus:

Newspapers, by their representatives, seek interviews to get matter for a "story," and out of the facts contained in the information furnished a "story" is made up. No doubt the reporters who gather this information write many facts in their reports, but the man in the swivel chair says: "That will not do. We must make it sensational, and we will dish it up to suit the sensational fanatics and this will not offend our religious higher-ups." An apt example is that of the New York "Post," which paper sent its reporter to get a "story" to publish about Jehovah's witnesses. The reporter was requested to put his questions in writing. That he did, and answers to his questions were written. When the story appeared in the New York "Post" it was entirely different from the facts furnished. The truth was entirely omitted and the very opposite was published.[4]

This was Mr. Rutherford's usual reaction to publications about the Witnesses. How could such response do anything but obstruct or stifle a thorough investigation of the movement?

In answer to a series of questions which I put to the Society, I received a letter expressing the same attitude. Although it was unsigned and bore only the official stamp of the Society, the writer was probably Mr. N. H. Knorr and not Mr. Rutherford, since Mr. Rutherford was presumably seriously ill in San Diego during the exchange of letters.

For your information, at no time in the past has any writer to our knowledge written a fair, unbiased account of Jehovah's witnesses' work or the Watch Tower Bible and Tract Society. . . . Any statements which you might make concerning the Society would be only your own ideas and not necessarily facts. . . . Men, stating their motives to be identical with yours and making statements to us that they wanted to write the truth, have been furnished the facts; but they have never published them. Our experience shows that reporters and writers gather information which they straightway refuse to print and instead print many falsehoods against us.

Considering the number of unsuccessful efforts to obtain accurate information from its officers, it may be safely concluded that such reticence justifies impartial observers in describing the organization as a "secret

---

[4] Rutherford, *The Theocracy*, p. 57.

society." To my knowledge, Mr. Rutherford's statement of the usual procedure of those seeking information about the Jehovah's Witnesses is unreasonable and misleading. It constitutes the standard "front" of the organization and, rightly or wrongly, a group which consistently hides facts that are basic to an understanding of it is likely to be regarded with suspicion. One reason frequently cited by officers for not telling more about the group is the hostility of Roman Catholics. To what extent, however, this hostility is invited by the Witnesses and distorted out of all proportion will be discussed later. In the present situation the danger does not seem to be objective.

As we have seen, the secretive attitude of the leaders is shared by the followers. One Witness, the leader of a local Company, said that he did not even care what the organization leaders did with the money collected or how they chose to operate, so long as they permitted him to continue serving. He would not allow a survey of the members in his group until he inquired of the central organization as to the advisability of permitting it—a matter of three weeks. The answer naturally was in the negative.

One technique widely used by the Society to discourage investigations is to stretch correspondence and contacts over a long period. For example, when I first tried to interview Mr. Covington, he asked me to call later for an appointment. Before doing so I asked the American Civil Liberties Union to send Covington through its counsel in charge of Witness affairs a statement as to my purpose and reliability. When I telephoned a week later, Mr. Covington said that he was unable to arrange an appointment at that time because he was preparing to leave the city for a period of days. He asked that I call him in about a week. When the week passed, I did so, only to be asked to call two weeks hence, "as work was pressing." After some weeks of this kind of stalling, I asked: "Am I right in assuming that you are willing to make an appointment with me to discuss the legal affairs of the Society?" He answered that he was not interested in making an appointment with me or any other investigator. This meant that I had to begin again from the beginning. The length of time needed, however, for reaching anyone of importance in the organization tends to destroy the initial enthusiasm and, in most cases, tires out the investigator.

It is for these several reasons that a detailed, scientific statement about the nature of the membership of the Jehovah's Witnesses cannot be made. Certain generalizations are possible, however, which may throw some light upon the character of the membership. A few aspects of the composition of the membership can be ascertained, although the report upon them must be regarded as tentative.

The Jehovah's Witnesses seems to appeal to few professional people. Some physicians appear to have been converted to the movement and they are regularly on duty during international conventions to attend Witnesses who fall ill. Few of these doctors consider the cult as a substitute for their profession; generally they regard it simply as "their religion," not allowing it otherwise to affect their daily lives. Several lawyers also have joined the cult, but these have been usually lawyers with small practices. Since the organization has been constantly in need of lawyers to defend Witnesses who have fallen foul of the law, some of the converts are employed on the legal staff at the central headquarters, and others in various centers elsewhere in the country.

From the beginning, a few Witnesses have been recruited from the Protestant ministry and the Roman Catholic priesthood. Mr. Russell used the high prestige-value attached to the ministerial function as a means of convincing early converts that his movement was sound. In the early issues of *The Watch Tower* he printed numerous testimonial letters written by ministerial converts. One minister said that after reading the material published by the Society he was convinced that "the dear old Methodist Episcopal Church is a part of the 'Image of the Beast,' and while I love it much, I love Christ Jesus more, and must obey God rather than man." In carrying out what he believed to be the command of Jehovah, this preacher severed his official relations with the Methodist Church and became a Pioneer.[5] Converted clergymen include not only Methodists, but also Lutherans, Baptists, Seventh Day Adventists, Episcopalians, and so on. There are even a few former Roman Catholic priests.

The general attitude of the Witnesses in their meetings toward members of the professions suggests their own social status. One Witness Pioneer reported in a house meeting that she had canvassed a number of offices, among them one of a physician. Since she came at a time when he had no patients in his office, the doctor listened to her description of her work, and after hearing her story bought almost a dollar's worth of the literature for his office. This experience the woman called "thrilling beyond words." During another meeting a Witness, in relating his

[5] *Watch Tower*, June, 1882.

experiences as a missionary for the movement in South America, made special mention of the lawyers with whom he had come in contact. He said that the lawyers were "very learned," but that they did not understand the Bible. He took delight in telling how he had confused them with biblical references, making one of them so angry that he took off his shoes and threw them at the retreating Witness.

Many of the Witnesses are poor and some are unemployed. Some take up the Pioneer work because they have lost their regular jobs; others, even though unemployed, cannot become Pioneers because of family responsibilities. The Jehovah's Witnesses soothes them by offers of large helpings of "pie in the sky." These unemployed become attached to the Witness theology and work, and find such compensatory joy that they forget about regular employment. As one of them said: "I have no work now, but if I were offered thousands in money for exchange for the truth, I would not part with it. If I do not have bread, let me at least have these studies." [6] When they cannot pay for the literature, the Society sends it free to those who send in their names.

Although Stanley High [7] states that the "Jehovah's Witnesses look like average Americans,—as, in fact, they are," my own observations lead me to think that the preponderant majority of them are not even "average," but noticeably under average in terms of social and economic privilege. In applying the test for measuring social status prepared by Professor F. Stuart Chapin of the University of Minnesota, I have found that the greater number of Witnesses whom I have studied fall into what he terms "relief cases, poverty," and "working-men." Naturally I have found some Witnesses who rank above "average" on such a scale, but these, often Company leaders, are few in number. My findings, however, were not of such a nature that they can be accepted as statistical evidence.

Women comprise a large part of the Witness membership, although perhaps not so large as among other Christian churches. In general the churches of the United States are predominantly filled with women. There are numerous contributing factors: men are "the breadwinners" and therefore do not have spare time or energy beyond their work to devote to activities of the church; the type of religious experience which the churches offer is basically feminine in its appeal. These same factors are apparent in the composition of the Witness membership, but, I think,

[6] *Ibid.*, Nov., 1922.   [7] "Armageddon, Inc.," *Saturday Evening Post*, Sept. 14, 1940.

to a lesser degree. The idea of the impending doom of civilization grips the minds of many men Witnesses so intensely that they willingly spend many hours beyond their regular employment in seeking to convert others through door-to-door service. Many of the appeals in the Witness movement, moreover, are basically masculine—fighting the enemy, protecting "the little flock," and so on—and men are the leaders. Women's place is "among the women," except when house-to-house calls are to be made. They gather together sometimes in the afternoon, much as do other women at their "bridge clubs," to talk over their experiences in the work, usually aided by tea and cookies.

Among the Witnesses may be found many elderly people, largely attracted by the theological conception of the afterlife. No one, according to correct Witness theology, will have to undergo the experience of death. In reality, death is merely a "becoming asleep." When a person "awakes" after death, he will find a perfectly formed world from which all evil is removed and where the fullest expression of his personality is permitted. Elderly Witnesses like particularly to stress the notion that in this perfect after-world all elderly people will become young, will be given new powers, and will take their places among the youth. Appealing also is the fact that the Witness theology has dropped completely all theories of eternal torment. If anyone believes in the Witness theology as a whole he will believe that every Witness is assured of life in the perfect after-world, and also that no circumstances can keep him from it. Some elderly people who have been members of other religious groups find that the creed of the Witnesses is much more favorable to old age than are those of the churches. Even a minister who had preached for years the reality of eternal torment came to believe, under the influence of Witness literature, that the doctrine was unscriptural. He speaks of the extent to which his changed beliefs affected his relationship to the denomination in which he had been a minister:

I am now sixty-three years of age. For some time I was a minister of the Protestant Methodist Church, but the study of the Scriptures led me farther from their creed. I finally withdrew, and for the last eighteen years have stood on the outside of the nominal churches. They have desired me to unite again, but I could not join with any sectarian organization. I felt and still feel called upon to come out from among them and be separate.[8]

[8] *Watch Tower*, July, 1883.

Some of the more elderly Witnesses have told me that they first became interested in religion in their old age because then they had time to read.

The movement also has great appeal to foreign-speaking groups in this country. The fact that the Society prints its literature in about seventy-eight languages provides Witnesses with the means of distributing literature to many who cannot read English. From the foreign-speaking groups, therefore, the Witnesses gain many converts. Local Companies are eager to hold meetings in foreign languages if there is a sufficient number of persons who desire them. The Society encourages its workers to give special consideration to the foreign-language areas in large cities and appoints specially qualified Pioneers to these areas: "I find that the brethren are not sufficiently alert to the opportunities among the foreigners in their town." [9] Probably no other religious group in this country, with the exception of the Roman Catholic Church, spends as much energy in ministering to the religious needs of foreign-speaking groups.

The Jehovah's Witnesses also contains a striking number of Jews, recruited from among those who consider themselves spiritual outcasts from formal religious organizations—they cannot maintain the orthodox faith of their fathers; they cannot become members of Christian churches. Seeking to preserve the values of their special heritage and yet hoping for a basic spiritual union with all people, they find themselves isolated religiously. To these the Jehovah's Witnesses appears inviting. The word "Jehovah" in the popular title of the organization has an especial appeal. The fact that many of the theological conceptions of the Witness movement are derived from the Old Testament also has some influence. A Jewish leader of a local Company told me that he had been reared by strictly orthodox parents, had been taught Hebrew "until it made my ears stand up," knew the complex ritualistic forms of Jewish orthodoxy, and yet felt that he was not "religious." When he reached the teen age he drifted away from the orthodoxy of his childhood, thereby greatly displeasing his parents. Later, when he heard the message of the Witnesses, he was converted; he believes that it retains all the worth-while emphases of his childhood (although in altered form), along with all that is worth while "out in the world." One such convert wrote to Mr. Rutherford about one of his books:

[9] *Ibid.*, March, 1914.

I do not believe that a Jew in the truth, enlightened by God, could have written the book with more wisdom in respect to Jewish prejudices or points of view than you, beloved Gentile, have done, moved by the love of the children of Abraham.[10]

The most pleasing part of the Witness belief to many Jewish followers is that which declares the Jews to be something of a superior people even among the believers. This attitude tends to give them a sense of unique prestige in the group. The Jews, according to the Witness theology, will be the first people to be blessed by Jehovah when the perfect world is established. The rest of the peoples of the earth will be blessed afterwards, but through the mediation of the Jews.[11] I have heard in meetings various non-Jews make deferential statements about the Jews present, such as, "I know that I shall not be chosen of the Lord before Brother 'Jew.' "

The question is often asked: How many Witnesses are there? To this there can as yet be no accurate answer. From its inception the movement has kept no membership lists, as far as public knowledge goes. The reason usually given for this is that, unlike the churches, the organization does not depend ultimately upon membership for its maintenance. Jehovah, according to the Witnesses, willed the existence of the movement and maintains it by his power. Aside from the fact that Jehovah's determination relieves them from worrying about counting members, the Witnesses say that the keeping of extensive records is costly in time and may induce believers to think more about the numbers on the rolls than about true service through the "witness" work.

Mr. Russell did not stress the idea of "numbers" because he felt that the coming end of the world made the building of a large organization unnecessary. It was his opinion in those early years—and he so warned his flock—that they would "decrease in influence and numbers . . . before the close of 1910." [12] Instead, however, the number of adherents increased, although the rate of increase has never been revealed. Slowly, through the years following the group's birth, new members were added until, at the death of the founder, thousands claimed themselves as true believers. During this period (from 1872 to 1916) contributions rose from zero to about $200,000; between 1916 and 1935 (the last year in which a financial statement was made public) they had risen to about

---

[10] *Ibid.*, March, 1927.   [11] Russell, *Studies in the Scriptures*, III, 249; I, 294.
[12] *Ibid.*, p. 243.

$250,000. Presumably the increase corresponds roughly with the rise in the number of the Witnesses.

There are very few strands of evidence which can be used to substantiate figures on the membership of the Jehovah's Witnesses. Official reports of the number of participants in the Memorial Supper (in which all believers partake) were given for some years until 1927. In 1925 approximately 90,000 participated, but two years later the number had decreased by about 2,000. The *Yearbook* of the Society for 1929 [13] states that the membership remained "about the same" as that of the previous year.

If I understand the history of the movement aright, the growth has been gradual, and by no means unusually accelerated in the past few years. I set this statement against the assertions put forth by the Society itself and by others who have observed the movement that a monumental acceleration has occurred in the past four or five years. At the time of his death, Mr. Rutherford, for example, claimed 2,000,000 followers. Many present-day Witnesses believe that the group recently has become greatly enlarged with new converts. A leader of a Company said that he thought that the number of Pioneers had increased in the last decade from 7,000 to 70,000. But there is no evidence. I interpret this statement as an attempt on his part to impress me with the strength of the movement.

Many Witnesses have been quick to criticize my use of the word "membership." They claim that one cannot become a "member" of the Jehovah's Witnesses; one can only become a "Jehovah's witness." This being so for them, the Witnesses recognize no ceremony of induction. Presumably the local Company does not keep a record of the Witnesses who attend its meeting, but in practice, each congregant is known and usually receives a postcard if he misses too many meetings. The local Company, as well as the central organization, also lists those who subscribe to the magazines, *The Watch Tower* and *Consolation*. I have found few Witnesses who were not subscribers to at least one of these magazines. In view of the scantiness of the evidence which I have been able to assemble, it seems advisable to make no guess as to numerical strength.

As to geographic distribution, I was encouraged by the hundreds of cases available in the files of the American Civil Liberties Union to at-

[13] Pp. 38–42.

tempt to chart the distribution of the Witnesses in this country, but here, too, the materials were not sufficiently reliable for my purposes. To my knowledge, there is at present no dependable means of discovering the exact extent and distribution of the Witness membership.

Regardless of social status, the Witnesses find the conversion experience of prime importance in their personal religious history. No matter how religious movements are judged, there are found within them persons whose needs are being met and whose hopes are being brightened, and for them the movement is sound and God-inspired. Within the Witness organization conversion is ascribed to many and sometimes even conflicting motives. People join for nearly as many reasons as there are individuals, and each person's story of his conversion is a valid proof of the vitality of the movement. There are not five or seven reasons why the Witnesses are as they are; the motives are legion. Cases scale from neurotic and psychotic states to those of the profoundly sane and healthy-minded. One Witness told me that he knew of a person who was paid $5 to accept the teachings of the group, but no such case has been verified and this in no sense represents the usual method of conversion.

Attached to the Jehovah's Witnesses, as to other religious groups of appreciable size, are some people who are disturbed mentally. Of course, such individuals do not impair the general value of the movement, but they should be cared for by other means. A woman Witness in Iowa was troubled because she was certain that she had commerce with demons from the spiritual world:

These demons seem in appearance to be beautiful, fascinating, but their character is vile. They do not desire to return to their "first estate" and say they will do more and worse evils now, so many minds being open. Well, they are having their trial now and if I must endure them for a time what a help I may be, in the coming age, to the poor mental and moral wrecks that have been made by them. My prayer is for grace to endure if God doesn't see fit to remove this torture. It may be valuable some day, otherwise I would destroy myself. Please excuse mistakes. A presence at my elbow is being fought with to get this written.[14]

Another Witness describes his condition as follows:

For seven years my brain has been in a vise, my head feeling like a rock weighing thousands of pounds—a dull, intense, drawing sensation—much

---

[14] *Watch Tower*, May, 1918.

worse than pain. My mind seems full of colors—green, yellow, blue, pink, and then suddenly the whole head seems to turn blood-red, producing hysteria, intense fear, and my mind becomes flooded with a total absence of faith in God.[15]

For what reasons these unfortunate people cling to religion cannot be known completely, but probably, in their condition, it provides one of the strongest—if not the strongest—ties which they have with the normal world.

Many Witnesses have been converted through experiences which seem unreliable to outsiders. Some Witnesses speak of opening the books of Mr. Rutherford, as did St. Augustine with the Bible, and of discovering sentences which they believe to be the direct voice of God to them. Others tell of their being convinced by mysterious means of the inherent truthfulness of the Witness message; for example, one Witness relates his experience with a ouija board:

I must confess that during the past couple of years I have been very unfaithful. I was anything but a humble, faithful follower of the dear Lord. I was serving sin and self. I had no desire for "present truth," still I had enough respect for it not to combat it. I did not meet with the dear brethren. In short I was very nearly trapped beyond hope of regaining freedom, in one of Satan's most successful devices, viz., Spiritism. I was induced to buy a "ouija board" just for amusement, but I dare say that that "amusement" almost lost me my "crown."

I spent all of my spare time in operating the "board" and became so skilled in its manipulation that it would perform rather difficult feats with the least solicitation. A neighbor having become fascinated upon seeing what "the little thing would do and say" purchased one for his own use. After trying to operate it without success, however, he came to me requesting that I try my hand. Strange as it may appear, it did all that I asked of it, and told me that it was a cousin to my board and "would do anything for me."

I can easily see that Satan, the chief operator of all ouija and planchette boards, was trying with all his might to get me more firmly into his clutches. My good morals were not entirely destroyed, however, and the adversary knowing this advised me to neglect my brethren and my Bible. I then asked whether the Jehovah's Witnesses writings are a correct interpretation of God's word. To this the reply came, "Yes, they are correct not only in doctrine, but in chronology as well." I then asked by what power the board was operated. It answered, "By evil, spirit, power." It further confessed to me that the spir-

[15] *Ibid.*

its who operated the board have no other mission than to hinder the Lord's people. It further stated that they took delight in buffeting, hindering, and endeavoring to snare the Society's leader and his co-laborers at the Bethel Home.

After thus confessing I concluded to destroy the board which I finally did. Before the destruction it pleaded for mercy, and tried every way to work on my sympathies. It told me that it would rather be given away or sold.

Before closing I wish to add that shortly after I bought the "ouija" I asked it if there was any possibility of my becoming as accomplished as "Hermann the Great." The answer came, "No." This answer rather surprised me, and I wanted to know why it had answered me thus. I used untold persuasion before I received the answer for the "No." And when I did get the answer, I got it a word at a time. The answer in substance follows: "Because God will not permit it." In order that I might not be mistaken, I enquired as to what "God" was meant. I was informed that it meant "the Almighty."

I need not explain that such an answer shocked me. It bewildered me to think that if Satan or any of his force ever told the truth it was then. Yes, I am a miracle of the dear Father's grace, through the wonderful merit of our blessed Lord and Saviour Jesus Christ. O how my yearning heart goes out to him for his love to me!—I the least of the least.[16]

Such approaches to religion do not seem unusual to the Witnesses, but rather, are considered as valid as any other, for Jehovah may use any circumstance to reach a person whom he wants in his work.

Some undergo conversion because they are responsive to the movement's claim to purity of religion. The literature abounds with arguments purporting to show that this is the final revelation of God and that all other religious organizations are Satan-inspired. Rutherford himself asserted that his movement had recovered "the original Christian basis" of religion.[17] Exemplifying this return to "original Christianity," the literature has consistently appealed to ancient manuscripts of the Bible rather than to the "inferior" common versions.[18] This appeal attracts many who yearn for a return to the true religion of Jesus. As one Witness said after her first visit to a Company meeting: "This meeting was the nearest approach in its character to the New Testament idea of the assembling of the saints that I have ever seen or heard." [19]

This stress on primitivism is also found in Mr. Rutherford's claim that the way of life pictured in the Old Testament indicates the will of Je-

---

[16] *Ibid.*, April, 1912.　　　　　　　[17] *Watch Tower*, March, 1889.

[18] Russell, *Studies in the Scriptures*, I, Preface.　　[19] *Watch Tower*, May, 1891.

hovah for the perfect society of the future. Rutherford described the future state as a time when every man would "sit under his own tree" and enjoy the simple fruits of his labor. The same nostalgia for the ancient past moves those with whom present-day society has dealt harshly.

Mr. Rutherford's dogma that the movement is superior to "nominal" churches and that it embodies the truest expression of biblical teaching carries great weight with many who have never been completely satisfied with their relationship to the churches:

I have a brother, a Doctor of Divinity, in the Methodist Church, and have always been told that I was called to preach the blessed glad tidings. But I have never felt satisfied with ORTHODOXY, although I have been a member for over twenty-five years. I threw out the doctrine of natural immortality FIVE years ago, the Trinity THREE years ago, and with the Emphatic Diaglott and the Bible and with other helps, have been feeling after the truth. I left the Methodist Church THREE years ago and though often asked to join that and others, never felt willing. . . . It [a Witness publication] satisfies my understanding and my longing spirit.[20]

Many Christians have been turned into Witnesses not only by the fact that the theology of the Witness movement claims to be the final expression of God's will, but also by the failure of the churches to care adequately for their spiritual charges. The Witnesses think that the churches lack to a marked degree the piety and godliness which they profess. They criticize the churches for their apparently inconsistent ways; Rutherford claimed that the churches desecrate Sunday even while preaching the sanctity of the day.[21] Moreover, the fact that the churches have split into a large number of bickering groups, none of which fully expresses the will of God, proves the inadequacy of denominational tenets. In a passage written by Mr. Russell and often quoted by the Witnesses may be found the group's attitude toward the sectarian, inconsistent nature of the various denominations:

As inquirers, we have two methods open to us. One is to seek among all the views suggested by the various sects of the church, and to take from each that element which might be considered the Truth—an endless task. A difficulty which we should meet by this method would be, that if our judgment were warped and twisted, or our prejudices bent in any direction—and whose is not—these difficulties would prevent our correct selection, and we might choose the error and reject the truth. Again, if we should adopt this as our

[20] *Ibid.*, May, 1882.   [21] Rutherford, *Hypocrisy*, pp. 51–52.

method we should lose much because the truth is progressive, shining more and more unto that perfect day, to those who search for it, and walk in the light of it, while the various creeds of the churches are fixed and stationary and were made so many years ago. And each of them must contain a large proportion of error, since each in some way, some important aspects, contradicts the others. This method would lead into a labyrinth of bewilderment and confusion.

The other method is to divest our minds of all prejudice and to remember that no one can know more about the plans of God than he has revealed in his Word, and that it was given to the meek and the lowly of heart, and as such, earnestly and sincerely seeking its guidance and instruction only, we shall by its great Author be guided to an understanding of it, as it becometh due to be understood, by making use of the various helps divinely provided.[22]

So the novice in religion is urged not to begin an eclectic procedure of discovering "the truth," but to rid himself of all prejudice and trust only in the Bible. Thus the Witness movement appeals to those who have not become intellectual sophisticates, for such could never believe that they had rid themselves of all prejudice. In actual practice, it attracts those who have experienced "the confusion of tongues" and have been unable to weld for themselves a solid, workable, living religious faith.

Uncertainty in regard to religious beliefs is created for some when they move from small country towns to large cities. Unable to find their way in the midst of a changed environment, they are easily led into new affections and affiliations. One Witness tells of his conversion as a result of the circumstances arising from such a move:

I joined a church in a small country town where the religious atmosphere seemed to be good. After some years I moved to a city and at once identified myself with the church there. I soon noticed the absence of the simplicity of religion and the prevalence of form and ceremony, including many kinds of entertainments to raise money. I grew dissatisfied, and though still loyal to the creeds, attended services intermittently.

Last August while homeward bound on the train I sat beside a lady who quietly handed me a folded magazine asking me that I read it and pass it on to others. Simply because her quiet manner attracted me, I said, "Yes." I did not think of the paper for several days and then felt too busy to take the time. This occurred several times until finally I remembered my promise to the woman and read the article, "Where are the Dead?" aloud to my companion. From the beginning our hearts and minds accepted all from cover to cover

22 Russell, *Studies in the Scriptures*, I, 11–12.

because the Bible was clearly proving them. O, the years of heart hunger and never to have heard of these writings nor the truth.[23]

The movement also catches many "spiritual vagabonds," that is, people who stray from one religious group to another without having a permanent interest in any. Some Witnesses have taken pleasure in reciting to me a long list of the religious affiliations which they had previous to coming into the Jehovah's Witnesses. Such a person wrote proudly from England to the Society headquarters in Brooklyn:

I joined the Church of England soon after I was converted [in early life], but a few months was enough there; then I joined the Wesleyans, but a little more than a year was enough; then I joined the "Brethren," and am still a member, but I do not think it likely to continue long, because when they know I deny the doctrine of the Trinity, as well as eternal TORMENT, I think my connection must cease of necessity.[24]

It is certain that many who come into the movement, however, leave it after a time for some new group which is offering tastier "spiritual delectables."

While there are cases in which persons have accepted the Witness message incontrovertibly upon first hearing it, the vast majority of persons reject it; only a few accept. Those who accept usually consider for some time before making up their minds, although, frequently, too lengthy consideration leads to rejection. The first Pioneer in the history of the movement says: "With shame I record that for three days I rejected these truths, almost wishing they were not scriptural and the very truth of God instead of joyfully welcoming them with grateful heart." [25] But, on the other hand, the period of consideration may become exceedingly long. A Witness said at the time of his conversion: "I have been seeing some of the truths for about seventeen years, but I did not have an understanding heart, I suppose, or else the sacrifices were too great." [26]

An occasional Witness may have an experience which so elevates and thrills him that he refers to it as a "second conversion." Some of these have told me that they have repeated "conversions" and that the normal Witness should progress in such a manner that his religious growth would seem like "one long, continuous conversion." The expression, "being converted," is used frequently among the Witnesses in this broader mean-

[23] *Watch Tower*, Nov., 1912. [24] *Ibid.*, Dec., 1881.
[25] *Ibid.*, June, 1881. [26] *Ibid.*, June, 1911.

ing: "This book [a Witness publication] has opened my eyes to some of the most blessed truths and its perusal has filled my heart anew with the love of God, and for the last few days, I have felt like a newly converted man." [27]

Some Witnesses cannot "date" the moment at which they became believers. Not all have cataclysmic religious experiences which stamp them as "new creatures." [28] For some the process of conversion demands a wholly revamped way of life; for others it simply means the addition of some novel theological conceptions or the attainment of a longed-for moral perfection: [29]

I wish I could see you and talk with you as my soul desires. I am so anxious for a pure heart—one from which emanates nothing but purity. As Peter said, not only my feet, Lord, but every word, thought and motive of the heart, I desire to have made pure and right. O, how I long for this, to be able to resist every form of evil! It is not possible for me to live with any evil in my heart. I want my environment to be clean; or rather, I want to be clean in my environment. [30]

This yearning is not always so fortified ethically that the seeker's life is channeled into socially helpful service. Commonly the Witnesses desire to be perfect merely for perfection's sake. Probably the majority are drawn to the movement because it proffers a means of eluding the very real evils of a world by which they have been roughly treated. They desire to be perfect, so that they may, by being so, withdraw from the world to live in their own self-created realm. [31]

I have found few Witnesses who are not disillusioned by life. They do not vote; they do not take part in community-service programs; they believe that the world has become so evil that it is not worth saving. This dominant motivation is expressed lucidly by the founder of the movement:

An important question arises regarding the duty of the saints during this trouble [the present unrighteous era], and their proper attitude toward the two opposing classes now coming into prominence. . . . The saint should take no part in that struggle. His consecration now was that he would strive to grasp and run for a higher, a heavenly prize, and hence he is weaned from earthly ambitions, and labors not for earthly things, except to provide things

---

[27] *Ibid.*, Jan., 1888.

[28] II Corinthians 5:17.

[29] Matthew 5:48.

[30] *Watch Tower*, Sept., 1892.

[31] "Peddlers of Paradise," *The American Magazine*, Nov., 1940.

DECENT and NEEDFUL; for his giving heed to the course and example of the Master and the apostles. Therefore, they have contentment with their godliness, not because they have no ambition, but because their ambition is turned heavenward and absorbed in the effort to lay up treasure in heaven and to be rich toward God; in view of which, and of their knowledge of God's plans revealed in his Word, they are content with whatsoever of an earthly sort God may provide. These can joyfully sing:

> "Content whatever lot I see
> Since 'tis God's hand that leadeth me."

We urge the saints, therefore, to abandon the strife and greed and vainglory and its discontent, and to strive for the higher riches and the peace they do afford. We would remind them of the apostle's words:

"Godliness with contentment is great gain; for we brought nothing into this world and it is certain that we can carry nothing out. And having (needful) food and raiment, let us therewith be content. But they that will (to) be rich (whether they succeed or not), fall into temptation and a snare, and into many foolish and hurtful lusts which DROWN (sink) men in ruin and destruction. For a root of all vices is the love of money (whether rich or poor), which some being EAGER FOR were led away from the faith and pierced themselves through with many pangs. But, thou, O man of God, flee from these, and be pursuing righteousness, godliness, faith, love, endurance, meekness; be contesting in the noble CONTEST of the faith, lay hold on everlasting life unto which thou wast called and didst make a noble covenant."

The poor world groans, not only under its real, but also under fancied ills, and especially under the discontent of selfishness, pride and ambitions which fret and worry men because they cannot fully satisfy them. Hence, while we can see both sides of the question, let us counsel those willing to hear to contentment with what they have, and to patient waiting until God in his due time and way brings to them the many blessings which his love and wisdom have provided.[32]

This is the type of religion which Karl Marx called "the opiate of the people," and such it is, for it drugs the believer into a pitiable complacency about the evils which infest our personal and collective lives. It acts further as a drug in that more and more of it is needed as time progresses. The frailty which some believers profess in the face of evil prohibits any attempt toward social amelioration. Thus is the cry of one

---

[32] Russell, *Studies in the Scriptures*, I, 338–341.

Witness to be regarded: "Tears come to my eyes when I consider how frail we are, and that the great Creator of the universe condescends to use us to praise him." [33] Not all Witnesses, however, confess to any such frailty. Some who talk about it while in the company of other Witnesses never let it be known when engaged in service work among outsiders. Others feel that the world has no power over them, but consider themselves superior to all events and persons. In general they agree with Nietzsche, but with different meaning: "All the values on which mankind now fixes its highest aspirations are decadence-values." Extreme emphasis upon the complete sovereignty of Jehovah accounts in part for this feeling of the Witnesses, but their concentration upon "heavenly" themes serves also to distract them and to minimize social and personal dangers. I asked a Witness whether in walking down the street he ever looked upon the passing people with pity because they did not understand "the truth." He said that he often did. He stated further that this feeling came about because he thought he had, unlike them, "solved the problem of life."

Some Witnesses take delight in displaying resentments toward those they consider to be inferior; thus church members and unbelievers are inferior because they do not accept "the truth." One Witness said: "I praise God that he has enabled me to follow him, and now I have Catholics and Protestants alike for enemies." [34] Another Witness told me that he liked to sell the Society's magazines on the streets for that allowed him to see unbelievers sneer at him. Their sneers did not disturb him because he knew that all unbelievers would be "eternally destroyed." Generally the unbeliever is thought of as one who has not seen the proper light—as though blinded. [35] Witnesses also have stronger names for those who do not accept their message.

Sometimes the feeling of superiority is expressed, but to a lesser degree, toward members of their own group. The newly converted believer is coddled by the older Witnesses with reasonable pride, and often the one who has been instrumental in making a conversion is not bashful about describing his persuasive ways even in the presence of the new believer. Some older Witnesses pride themselves upon their superior knowledge of the Witness theology, of the Bible, or of the works of Mr.

---

[33] *Watch Tower*, June, 1931.   [34] *Ibid.*, June, 1885.

[35] A Witness on trial for heresy in a Baptist church declared to the church court: "I believe that many of you are Christians, but blinded." *Watch Tower*, Jan., 1889.

Rutherford. In this sense they echo Sir Joseph's words which, in his situation, describes the same feeling: "The British sailor is any man's equal, excepting mine." [36]

Persecution has been a strong factor in the success of the movement by bringing the plight and the message of the Witnesses to the attention of many people. Any religious movement that becomes a target of abuse attracts sympathetic defenders, those who champion "the underdog," in much the same way as one cheers at a baseball game for the losing team. One Witness says concerning the factors contributing to his conversion: "All my life my heart's best sympathies have been on the side of oppressed humanity and I have turned neither to the right hand nor to the left for crowns or favors." [37] Mr. Rutherford's presentation of the movement as one constantly and bitterly persecuted has led seasoned Witnesses as well as new converts to take up the gauntlet with amazing courage and determination.

The stern theology of the movement attracts many who have no developed religious outlook, who in Witness parlance are "infidels." In brief, the appeal is to those who in Edwin Arlington Robinson's description say:

> I cannot find my way: there is no star
> In all the shrouded heavens anywhere.

The Jehovah's Witnesses have found their "star." Moreover, it is not veiled in some far-distant haze, but is a living authority, proclaiming itself as the beacon to the appointed way. The fact that this group looks with aversion upon all organized religion, all churches, and all creeds appeals to the "infidels." The movement enforces an iron-clad and rigid discipline which the search-weary unbeliever docilely accepts. Witnesses are encouraged to do their service work especially among this group: "I find some infidels who hearing the truth, are beginning to think that the Bible is true, and some have accepted the truth and are telling the good news to others showing that the Bible is a reasonable book when understood." [38] The appeal to infidels is particularly effective when a biblical background is present. One Witness told me that he had been reared to believe strictly in the inerrancy of the Bible and in a hard, Calvinistic theology. When he reached his early twenties and visited various denominational churches he found that each preached a different

---

[36] *Pinafore*, Act I.   [37] *Watch Tower*, Nov., 1895.   [38] *Ibid.*, Nov., 1883.

doctrine. So shattered was his faith in the Bible and in his theology, that for some years he was without any religious faith whatsoever. During this period his aged mother constantly chided him on his newly adopted attitude and said that she could not love a son who did not believe in the Bible and in God. One day the young man was approached by a Witness who told him that the Jehovah's Witnesses hated all religions, but loved the Bible and God. The young man was converted shortly thereafter, much to the comfort of his mother.

Another example of experience of this same sort comes from a former officer in the Salvation Army:

For ten years an officer in the Salvation Army engaged in "rescue" work, my heart had been terribly burdened, not only with my own inability to live up to the divine standard, but also with the apparently hopeless condition of others less favored than myself.

Dissatisfied for a long time, and having lost almost all faith in God and in the Bible, I did not know what to do or what to believe. In my extremity, I continued to pray like this, "O, Lord (if there is any God) help me! Help me now! Send me a little light (if there is any light). Let me know what is the truth (if anything is true)." And in his infinite love he answered that prayer sending me the Jehovah's Witnesses books. Since that time the language of my heart is expressed exactly in the words of the hymn beginning:

"My life flows on, in endless song." [39]

The Jehovah's Witnesses has been able also to attract those who have foreboding thoughts about death. Some who have suffered loss in their own families, and who have not previously worked out a satisfying philosophy of life, find the experience devastating to their faith in God and the church. The Witness theology brings to such people contentment about death, about the nature of the afterlife, and especially about the scaring doctrine of hell-fire. The churches do not always explain these somber doctrines satisfactorily, and as a result even some faithful church members find the Witness theology more convincing than their own.

Were it not for one of the Jehovah's Witnesses I would today be in the depths of despair. I buried my dear little three year old daughter one year ago; and after three months of grieving, with no minister able to give me real comfort, one of these Witnesses stopped at my door and with a beautiful smile told me of God's wonderful purpose. And to think that I had been searching for the truth for twenty years in the churches.[40]

[39] *Ibid.*, Nov., 1913.　　　　　　　　[40] *Ibid.*, April, 1934.

The believer does not need to spend his present energies worrying about his future, for Jehovah has arranged future events so that the end will be good; therefore, he must simply trust in Jehovah both in life and in death. "I have always dreaded dying, but if its [a Witness publication] conclusions are correct (and it at once impressed me so), I think I want to die—anything to be with Christ." [41]

There are also persons who continually worry about the state of life after death. By them the existence of a literal heaven and hell is taken for granted. Many can visualize these places very much as some can visualize the Devil.[42] To such literal-minded people the problem is especially pertinent to their present living, and to them the movement brings comfort in its proclamation that there is no hell. The wicked will be totally destroyed at the great battle of Armageddon, but the righteous will live on. Only those who disbelieve will be destroyed; believers will be saved from the great destruction. This conception of the efficacy of belief comes as a relief to those who have been worried about the future life. One woman described her conversion and its effect, saying that, having accepted the Witness doctrine, "it was only a short time before I had the hell theory cleared up." [43] Another Witness was happy to learn (erroneously) that the doctrine appears neither in the Old nor the New Testaments of the Bible:

I have been a member of the ————— church for a number of years, but have felt often that we did not get all of the gospel. I have always been taught from infancy until now, and I am over forty years old, that this life is only a probation, and that at death our eternal destiny was unalterably fixed, and it nearly took my breath away when I found that no such assertion was made either in the Old or New Testaments, and I am familiar with the Bible from Genesis to Revelation.[44]

The movement also appeals to those who are social outcasts. Like Marmeladov, in *Crime and Punishment*, these have "no place to turn." They have been battered about by a cruel world until they have lost their social identity. They are afraid to think for themselves, for such is not expected of them. They wander from pillar to post, sometimes fed, but often not. When these people accept "the truth" they are cared for by

[41] *Ibid.*, Jan., 1882.
[42] A Witness confesses: "I was afraid to go to bed at night for fear the Devil would take me by the leg. That may sound simple, but it is a fact." *Watch Tower*, Aug., 1903.
[43] *Watch Tower*, Sept., 1912.   [44] *Ibid.*, Jan., 1888.

the Witnesses. They are given a definite place in the Company; this lifts them in their feeling of personal worth and gives them a degree of social prestige. They become an indissoluble part of a world-wide movement, and as such they share in its possessions and hardships.

On the whole, those who become Witnesses are unappreciative of mystical experiences. The converts are generally people who want a religion which will help them with their problems in a mundane way; seldom do they require "union with God." But mystical experiences do occur. Probably they occur in every conversion experience. Commonly they are described by the Witnesses as necessitating a period of preparation, and, finally, a "breaking forth in joy."

Really I hardly know myself for joy. For some time past I have been dimly conscious that blessing was hovering over me, because I have been going through DEEP waters, and I could not account for it. I asked my fellow-believers if they were used to such wrestling as I was experiencing, and they knew nothing of it. I see now that the fallow ground was being broken up to receive the GOOD SEED. O how I praise him for the truth he has given me, and in what a way too.[45]

When such experiences come to the believer, they are usually accompanied by a feeling of intimate union with the divine, such as is described by Robert Browning in his "Pauline":

> My God, my God, let me for once look on thee
> As though nought else existed, we alone.

In these moments the believer sometimes feels himself morally equal to God: "I am not aware that there is any inharmony between my will and the will of God." [46] A leader of a local Company thought that the main reason why he joined the movement was his desire "to be one with Jehovah and to know it for a certainty." For those who fear the coming destruction of the end of this age, union with Jehovah is the one unchanging security in a changing world.

---

[45] *Ibid.*, May, 1881. [46] *Ibid.*, Dec., 1891.

The Ways of the Witness

MANY OF THE WITNESSES who experience conversion expect and achieve definite results, for, even as Homer declared, the gods listen to those who obey them. With inner regeneration the Witnesses undergo a social orientation which affects almost every phase of their lives. They feel that the very nature of their lives has been altered. "I am a changed man." [1] For their former evil selves a new form and spirit have been substituted. Sometimes the change of character becomes so real to the initiate that he thinks of himself as constantly acting upon a divine plane: "I find it is like Christ Jesus—to be just to all men. O, praise his name." [2]

Some converts express a feeling of release from a type of slavery that is usually referred to as a compulsion of "the flesh." The new-found freedom brings a sense of emotional release which is evident in such ecstatic utterances as: "What I want to tell you is this. I am FREE. The TRUTH has made me free." [3] Those having this experience are impelled to share it with others: "I love the truth; I am made free by it; and I love to tell it to others; and, O, when I find a hearing it does me so much good." [4]

A feeling of unworthiness may also accompany the conversion experience. In such cases the neophyte is usually deeply impressed with the guilt of his misdemeanors and with the transcendent love of Jehovah. The feeling of unworthiness may be intensified until the convert's every act is accompanied by a sense of guilt, but more often it tempers and is tempered by other emotions and a balance is achieved. Natural expressions of humility are recurrent: "Sometimes I cannot keep back the tears as I think of the abounding wealth into which I have entered." [5] With the feeling of indebtedness to God goes the thought of the necessity for loyal service: "What a privilege it is to work for our God." [6]

As already suggested, the conversion experience is spoken of as bringing great "riches" to the believer. The convert's earthly income becomes unimportant in the light of the heavenly riches which he has glimpsed. For persons lacking a sufficient supply of the necessities of life, conversion is realized especially in terms of money: "In this world's goods I am a poor man, but I am richer with the glorious knowledge of God's Word that has come to me than I ever hoped to be rich." [7]

[1] *Watch Tower*, Jan., 1888. [2] *Ibid.*, April, 1893. [3] *Ibid.*, Jan., 1893.
[4] *Ibid.*, Sept., 1892. [5] *Ibid.*, June, 1911. [6] *Ibid.*, Nov., 1895.
[7] *Ibid.*, Nov., 1915.

The new faith becomes exciting and full of life for the believer. All he had formerly known of religion merely serves to accentuate the superiority of his new beliefs. As one Witness says: "O, how dull and blunted does now appear the common method of Christian instruction." [8] The written page becomes perchance Jehovah's means for disclosing his purposes; the spoken voice becomes the medium of the Deity to speak to the believer. All life is filled with the intimate presence of Jehovah. Every common flower is aflame with God:

He has arranged a mass of concurring events well calculated to increase our faith. I am reminded of this every day. I find men fulfilling prophecy; saying and doing many things, freely and voluntarily, which they have not the remotest idea had any connection with God or heaven, and yet which is of such a nature, or has such a relation to things which are of interest to the child of God who is watching closely every indication of the presence of the Lord, as to impress him forcibly with the thought that he is even AT THE DOOR. [9]

The new faith is understandable to the believer because of its simplicity.

It is a relief to turn from the crooked and tangled reasonings of men, to the simple clear Word of God. Its statements are full of heavenborn power to those who receive them. I believe with all my heart that a little Scripture is worth a great deal of reasoning; and I am so glad man's reasoning cannot alter God's Word. [10]

The Bible, being the textbook of religion, is to be studied diligently. The theological system of the Jehovah's Witnesses contains "answers" to all questions; therefore, there truly can be no doubts, not even those which are the expression of a growing mind; every doubt whatsoever is Satan-inspired.

The Witness views his religion not as a spontaneous, growing experience, but as a complete theological system, which claims to subsume under some one of its precepts every question that life can ask. So Russell conceived it, and his attitude has carried over to the present day. Sometimes a Witness calls his religion "progressive"—meaning that it is not a "closed system"—but to most of the Witnesses a "progressive" religion in that sense is just what they do not want. Throughout its history the Jehovah's Witnesses has expressed its official attitude on the matter in a passage in one of the first works of Mr. Russell: "Be it known that no

<hr>

[8] *Ibid.*, Jan., 1882.   [9] *Ibid.*, May, 1881.   [10] *Ibid.*, Jan., 1880.

other system of theology even claims, or ever has attempted, to harmonize in itself EVERY statement of the Bible; yet nothing short of this we claim for these views." [11]

The Witness message, however, is not always received as a totally new revelation. To many, the experience of becoming believers does not lead to any great change of views or habit. But the latter do not take a prominent place in the meetings and do not attempt otherwise to capitalize upon their conversion experience. They are hence not representative. Not all of the conversions are permanent. When any new religious doctrine is announced, then, in Longfellow's words, "many are amazed and many doubt." Sometimes doubts occur at the time the message is first being heard, with the result that the hearer never even affiliates himself with the movement. Again, doubts occur after the hearer has accepted the message, on occasion, after conversion, when the effects of the original experience have faded out. Such Witnesses frankly admit that the conversion experience has left them "dry." One of them wrote to the Society's leaders:

I feel no nearer to God now than I did when I first wrote you about my trouble; it rather gets darker all the time. O, I do feel wretched. I feel just as if I had been a deceiver. The more I think about the past the worse I feel about it.[12]

Some of those who come to doubt after conversion speak of searching for another religious group in which they might be able to find the desired peace and satisfaction. Occasionally such Witnesses write to their leader of their condition. One backsliding Witness thought that his doubts were due to pride; he said that he could not give himself over to any movement completely, because he felt that such a surrender would rob him of his individuality. When the Society's leader replied, telling him that he would never achieve happiness and security until he would surrender himself completely to "the truth," the Witness answered as follows:

This [losing of faith] came about gradually; and now I see that I was losing the Lord's favor gradually, although I did not notice for some time, nor realize the cause until in my despair I wrote to you. When once I realized that pride was at the bottom of it, I was enabled to trace the matter to its true source as well as to see the horribleness of my own position. Indeed, while I see the truth clearly, I confess that in my restless state, I began to look

[11] Russell, *Studies in the Scriptures*, I, 348.   [12] *Watch Tower*, Dec., 1892.

around for something else—seeking rest and finding none. Truth began to get valueless. It lost its power of influence over me. I verily believe that I was nearing the condition mentioned in the parable as "outer darkness." But now, since I see and confess my error and am earnestly seeking the Lord, the truth again has a powerful influence over me; but I fear so much that I have been so unfaithful that the Lord will never own or use me again.[13]

Serious doubts are not uncommon even among those who have been Witnesses for a long time. Many who had been associated with Mr. Russell from the beginning of the movement came to doubt the teachings of Mr. Rutherford. Usually the difficulty centered on the manner in which Rutherford carried out the program instituted by the founder. Doubts also arose when he failed sufficiently to stress beliefs that were central to Russell's theology:

As is the case generally, my troubles all grew from a very small beginning consisting of hints and half-veiled suggestions coming in the most part from those I have reason to believe are truly sons of God. Many half-formed doubts had found place in my mind, and then suddenly came the deluge. The first suggestion, coming like a flash of lightning, was that Brother Rutherford had denied the ransom. This was followed by suggestions along many lines, backed by Scripture quotations and references to old "Tower" articles which seemed to show that the present teaching of the Society was contrary to the fundamentals taught by Brother Russell.[14]

Some Witnesses were led to doubt certain tenets of the movement by a really thorough study of the Bible. Although the Bible is claimed by the Witnesses as their final authority, they seldom use it, except to call the roll of myriads of supposedly-supporting verses. The Bible is used in house meetings more frequently than in Watch-Tower meetings, but merely to bolster the writings of Mr. Rutherford. Not very often do Witnesses offer to sell Bibles to the people whom they meet in their service work. Mostly they assume that everyone knows what the Bible teaches with regard to every doctrinal subject; they also assume that they themselves know what the Bible teaches. Therefore, when a Witness undertakes a serious study of the Bible without recourse to the "Bible helps" provided by the Society, he may come to question the theology of the movement. Occasionally his doubts are denounced by himself as tools of Satan, used to lure believers from the organization and as such

[13] *Ibid.*   [14] *Ibid.*, June, 1925.

are fought off (often with the help of other Witnesses), as in the following instance:

Then came great illumination of mind—things seemed to be as clear as crystal. I seemed to be lifted above the cares of life and while I was conscious of great conflict, yet I was grandly calm with what seemed perfect poise. Many wonderful interpretations of Scripture flooded my mind, so ingenious that it seemed that they must be true. In fact, I believe that many were true, perhaps used as a bait to lure me on. Satan surely is assuming the part of "an angel of light." Sleep seemed unnecessary; food only a matter of little concern.

Then came the suggestion that perhaps the Lord was about to use me in some way, some very wonderful and honorable way. Surely, had not God used a dumb ass? ALL THE TIME I felt his love and favor and I earnestly prayed that I might be led into the truth and not swallow up the error, also that I might not injure any of the little ones; and he answered my prayers. By the aid of some dear brethren and the letter sent me by Brother Rutherford, the Lord delivered me from the snare of the fowler.[15]

Becoming a Witness is not a simple matter to any Witness who takes his religious life seriously. I have met some who have felt that they were entirely in sympathy with the teachings of the movement, but thought that they could not call themselves true believers until they managed to achieve some goal which they had set for themselves. The goals are usually of a "spiritual" character; many are centered in the "ego problem," or what has been called "the selection of the dominant self." The Witnesses, like others, find that they do not have absolute control over themselves, that they are not, properly speaking, one integrated self. They have told me that at times they can picture themselves as members of other religious groups and this causes them to wonder about the validity of their own religious experience. Some have said that they could wake up in the morning doubting all of their Witness beliefs if they permitted themselves to do so, but seldom do they take this step. Like members of other communions, they find that they have to deal with moods of elation and despair; they must confront success and failure in their service work; they must be alert in spite of fatigue. These variable factors in the daily routine tend to divert some Witnesses from the single-mindedness of faith demanded of them. It also tends to remind them that no experience can transport them from the ordinary world in which they

[15] *Ibid.*

live. Variations in mood made one person hesitate to become a Witness until he could solve his problem, and after he thought he had solved it, the dilemma persisted so that he felt his conversion had been in vain:

I had always tried to keep self under, but failed, till at last considering God's promises that his grace is sufficient for us, I took the step and made outwardly the confession that I would reckon myself dead, and accept God's way and will instead of my own. Looking back now I see that I again failed.[16]

Sometimes Witnesses begin to doubt the theology of the movement after meeting discouragement in their service work. Generally, persecution endured in the work tends to strengthen the faith of the worker, but occasionally it may set him to questioning. One veteran Witness was especially struck by the apparent ineffectiveness of his service work: "I have written much upon the heavenly theme, as well as spoken much, but to all appearances to no avail. I appeared to address an unappreciative people." [17] Occasionally a Witness becomes discouraged because of the attitude of fellow workers. A Pioneer who had lived for a time at Bethel House in Brooklyn told me that the other workers there were so proud of their superior knowledge that he felt they were not primarily interested in "doing the Lord's will." This led him to wonder if the whole movement was false. He said that he did not regain his faith until he left the House and traveled about in the field.

But it is infrequent that a Witness is converted to some new communion and leaves the Jehovah's Witnesses. The Witnesses do count among their number many who are unstable in faith and wander about from one cult to another, ever in search of "the tree of life." If these become Witnesses, they take part actively in the field service for a time, but then drift into other religious groups such as Bahaism, New Thought, or the Unity Movement. Occasionally a Witness may leave the movement because of criticism by his friends. The charge is sometimes made that if those who study religion grow too interested in the subject, they may become mentally unbalanced. The application of this popular notion to Witnesses has caused some of them to question their own zeal and in a few cases to leave the movement entirely. One renegade Witness tells that he left the movement because of such pressure from his friends: "They called me a fool, and said that if I did not leave religion alone I would soon be in the insane asylum." [18]

[16] *Ibid.*, Dec., 1892.   [17] *Ibid.*, Sept., 1883.   [18] *Ibid.*, June, 1893.

Whenever a Witness leaves the flock his former companions speak of the subtle work of Satan upon those of weak faith. If secessions occur too frequently in a local Company, extra classes are set up to study the fundamental tenets of the movement; the Witnesses are warned "not to cast pearls before swine," that is, they should be more careful in the instruction of their converts. The breaking away of some Witnesses is explained on the grounds that they probably never did know "the truth": "It is a mistake to suppose that those without faith, and consequently justification, should be able to apprehend clearly the truth. It is not for such." [19]

The consequences of lasting conversion upon the Witnesses have been open to observation and study. Following his conversion, the believer enters upon a discipline designed to form him according to the image of the ideal Witness. He receives a new vocabulary, with new meanings, which in the course of time become habitual, and are the same for all. The Witnesses do not try to express their ideas in ways of their own, but employ fixed word patterns constituting the official parlance of the movement. Should any one not follow these patterns, his orthodoxy is quickly and seriously questioned.

Some of the word patterns have been employed since the movement's inception. One such is "the truth." This expression occurs for the first time in the official literature of the movement as early as 1895.[20] Since that time most true believers have called their conversion their coming into "the truth." Today the phrase is heard among Witnesses more often than the word "God."

"Jehovah" is also much more frequent in Witness conversation than the word "God." By "Jehovah," the Witnesses generally intend the theological attributes of the Old Testament "Jahweh." They rarely use "Jesus Christ" to signify deity. Their usual appellation for Jesus, moreover, is "Christ Jesus," with little stress upon his messianic nature.

The Witnesses seldom speak of "good" and "evil," but are inclined to personify whatever they mean by these terms as "Jehovah" and "Satan." In contrasting good and evil the Witnesses regularly use such institutionalized forms of expression as "Jehovah's organization" and "Satan's organization." The "good" social institutions consist solely of the Jehovah's Witnesses, while the "evil" always include the Roman Catholic Church, other churches, the American Legion—or just about

[19] J. H. Burridge, *Pastor Russell's Position*, p. 23.   [20] *Watch Tower*, Feb., 1895.

every organization other than the Jehovah's Witnesses. When the Witnesses speak of "Jehovah's organization," Jesus is often termed "Jehovah's executive officer"; the leaders of the opposing institutions are regularly called "overlords."

Among other characteristic phrases is "the theocracy." Introduced about 1939, it has become one of the dominant catchwords, and formed the title of a book published by Rutherford in 1941. All human history, say the Witnesses, shows that the only possible form of government under God is that of "the theocracy." As examples, they refer to the kingdom of Saul, David, and Solomon. This Old Testament type of theocracy is regarded as the one religious organization of society for the future. Increasingly the attention of the movement is becoming fixed on this slogan and its underlying concept.

A newly converted Witness can be distinguished by the infrequency of these clichés in his speech; he may have trouble in expressing his ideas, but the older Witness knows by rote most of the special vocabulary of the dogmas of his faith. Their verbal patterns remind one of Voltaire's words:

A fashionable invalid or doctor will take into his head to say that he has a soupçon of fever to signify that he has a slight attack; soon the whole nation has soupçons of colics, soupçons of hatred, love, ridicule. Preachers in the pulpit tell you that you must have at least a soupçon of God's love. After a few months this fashion gives place to another.[21]

Among the Witnesses, the fashion lasts much longer, usually five or ten years. Such phrases are repeated in meetings, at home, in the field service, and in prayers, and competence in their use is taken as a sign of spiritual maturity. Older Witnesses not only are skilled in this regard; they also intone their sentences in a way which immediately identifies them as "religious." The pious intonation is designed to impress the hearer. A new convert is not expected to use it well, but he is making poor progress if he does not quickly acquire it.

Besides endeavoring to realize in himself the ideal Witness, he must not only change his mode of speaking but must also "sever all relations with the world." A pious Witness wrote to Mr. Russell: "Will you kindly advise me in regard to severing my connection with the church of which I am a member? I feel as though I should not attend because I would be

---

[21] Voltaire, *Philosophical Dictionary* (New York, Alfred A. Knopf, 1924), pp. 182–183. Reprinted by permission of the publishers.

consenting to their teaching which I do not now believe." [22] In reply, Mr. Russell roundly criticized the churches as apostates from the Word of God. He declared that they profess one sort of morality and practice another. He likened them to the "anti-Christ" of the Book of Revelation, and declared that because they were so evil, the true believer must "come out from among them and be clean." This settled the debate as to whether the movement which Russell founded was to work within the framework of the churches, as Buchmanism has in recent years, or whether it should make itself a separate and distinct organization. Opposition to other churches is a condition of witnessing; all "true" Witnesses are expected soon after conversion to cancel their church membership, if they hold any: "Any attempt to remain in the organization or 'chariot' of the Lord and at the same time to support the wicked world, even with the unwise desire of lifting up the world, will meet with disaster." [23]

Some churches have felt bitter toward Witnesses who have canceled their membership, but more recently the attitude has been more tolerant. One Witness who wanted his church membership canceled received from his minister a letter stating that the request would be granted but that his name would still be kept on the church rolls because "we still want to claim your fellowship."

The task of financing the movement is promptly put up to the convert, for the ideal Witness must be generous. Since no collection is taken at the meetings, private giving is required. Witnesses may either contribute weekly by putting money in the collection boxes at the rear of the meeting halls, or may pledge a certain amount to be paid at stated intervals to the Company treasurer, or they may do both. There is no "envelop system" for regular giving, such as exists in many churches. The Society claims that tithing is an unnecessary burden upon the members, and reminds its followers of a "better doctrine," namely, that all of a man's possessions belong to Jehovah. Witnesses are enjoined to "live decently," and to give all surplus to God.[24] What percentage of yearly income the Witnesses contribute to the Society is not known, but it probably equals the tithe.

The ideal Witness must forgo the pleasure of hymn-singing, which is not encouraged by the Society. This was not always the case. As early as 1879 Russell published the *Songs of the Bride*, containing 144 "Scrip-

---

[22] *Watch Tower*, Jan., 1882.   [23] Rutherford, *Angels*, p. 63.
[24] *Watch Tower*, Nov., 1883.

tural hymns" commonly sung in the churches. These songbooks sold ordinarily for fifteen cents each, but were free to the poor. In 1896 members of the organization published a small collection of hymns all of which were composed by Witnesses. This book of twelve pages was called *Zion's Glad Songs of the Morning*. It was followed by several other songbooks (the last in 1927) made up of familiar tunes from regular church hymnals but with words to fit the theological framework of the Witness movement. But for some reason the Society frowned upon the practice, and today the Witnesses do not sing in their meetings, except at international conventions. It is strange that the Society does not recognize the value of singing as a unifying and stimulating activity. Witnesses do not sing, they say, because it "takes up too much time in these crucial times," yet they seem ill at ease without it. At house meetings hymns are sometimes sung after the meeting has been dismissed, but always with the implication that this is something unauthorized by the central organization. One Witness that I met had a son who had been an "excellent" singer before he became a Witness. The father said that it was a hard decision for the boy to give up his professional career, but the Lord "helped him to do it." A converted singer usually renounces his profession; it is likely "to start him thinking along different lines."

The newly converted Witness is urged by the older members to attend Model Study meetings and the house meetings in his neighborhood. When these meetings end, the neophyte may ask the small group such questions as occur to him, express his doubts, and thereupon receive "proper" answers. Although the older Witnesses pretend to answer all questions "openly," they do not in fact say anything which has not already been said by Mr. Rutherford.

For some time a newcomer is suspected of being a "spy." He does not find the other Witnesses relaxed and informal in his presence. They test him for sincerity; they ask many questions about his background and want to know in detail the nature of his real beliefs. If he successfully passes all tests, he is gradually admitted to greater comradeship. Within a period of two or three months, varying according to the situation, he is allowed to accompany an older Witness in the house-to-house canvassing. He subsequently attends Thursday evening meetings at a Kingdom Hall where he receives practical instruction in the methods employed in the service work. Following this, he again canvasses several times with an older Witness, until he feels adequately prepared to undertake the service work alone. At this point he is called a Company Publisher and takes on the responsibilities of that group—filing daily reports, and so on. When he becomes a Publisher he is considered "safe."

The mature Witness takes on certain definite habits and attitudes that mark him as a true believer. For example, he must not be a philanthropist, except to the Society. When I asked a group of Witnesses if they would contribute to a private institution for the aged, they refused. I reminded them that many elderly people are housed in institutions dependent in large part upon private contributions. If the contributions were not forthcoming, I told them, the lives of these old people would be seriously threatened. To this the Witnesses replied that they could not contribute. No matter how seriously the lives of the old people were endangered, it was more important for Witnesses to employ their resources in spreading the Witness message. Hence the organization is not officially concerned in caring for the needs of others. In 1924 the Society did ask for old clothes for the poor, but the event is unique.[25] The Witnesses believe that the course of history has been downward, that it has reached its lowest depths, and that nothing in our present world merits salvaging.

Officially the Witnesses follow the Fundamentalist Protestants in their stand against smoking and drinking liquor. They hold that these two practices have been proved evil by scientific experimentation, and are taboo not only to the believer by reason of their inherent impurity, but especially because the Bible specifically prohibits their use. The least indulgence in either is considered a "habit." Witnesses in rural areas denounce the "temperance" movement as condoning "moderation"; they refuse to support any "earthly" organization permitting anything short of "total abstinence." This means that if a Witness allows himself to smoke even once or to take any sort of alcoholic drink, even in medicines, he has sinned. The literature is replete with examples of persons who were "cured" of either drinking or smoking by their conversion.[26] In 1924 Mr. Rutherford announced that he strongly favored "the Prohibition Act."[27] While total abstinence prevails among Witnesses in rural areas and in small towns, and especially among those who have strong Fundamentalistic propensities, this does not hold true in the larger cities. In one home where I attended a house meeting, the host served "Swedish punch" after one meeting, and after another, served us coffee containing some sort of liquor. In this particular home, liquor was served after almost every Witness meeting. Sophisticates like these sometimes jibe at the provincialism of rural Witnesses.

Tobacco was forbidden to members of the Jehovah's Witnesses quite early. Many converts in those early days spoke of their desire to stop smoking, and many claimed that only by their conversion were they enabled to do so. Here is how a Witness of 1891 tells about his battle:

About a year ago, I asked the Lord in all sincerity and prayer to assist me in quitting the use of tobacco, and promised him in all good faith to use the money formerly spent for it in the advancement of his interests, as I now see it through the light that I have received. I had used tobacco for thirty years and often tried to quit it, but could not resist the strong desire for its use; but since I quit this time, with the help of the Lord, I have lost all desire for it, and only twice, shortly after quitting, have I had the least desire for it.[28]

In recent years smoking has become more common and in the rural areas some of the Witnesses chew tobacco. Russell's strictures were either forgotten or conveniently not applied. Some who had been with the organization since the old days have written to Mr. Rutherford protesting the extended use of tobacco among "younger" Witnesses. In order to appease these old-timers and to be in harmony with the original principles of the movement, Mr. Rutherford restated the Society's position on the use of tobacco, but in a much milder form. A Witness who smokes was not declared untrue to his religious beliefs; Rutherford even argued that the use of tobacco is "clean," and condemned it solely because the Witnesses "should have something better to do with their time and money."

Another of the original teachings which has lapsed into a "blue" law, although never officially denied, is that of "spiritual healing." The early literature refers to many cases of healing as the direct result of right belief. A father tells of his daughter who was nearing blindness from a seemingly incurable malady. He consulted as many physicians as he could afford, and with the financial aid of friends took the eighteen-year-old girl to a few "specialists." The latter declared she would never regain her sight but would grow progressively more blind. The father, in desperation, called in all "faith-healers" who cared to try a hand, among them a Christian Scientist. None, however, helped the girl. The despondent father resigned himself to the situation until he came in con-

[28] *Ibid.*, Sept., 1891.

tact with the Witness movement. Converted, he prayed for long periods that his daughter might be cured. After a while, the daughter began to see again and gradually regained her full sight. Of course, a miracle.[29]

The healing of "impossible" illnesses generally was considered miraculous and bound the healed person forever to Jehovah and his organization, the Jehovah's Witnesses. The following case of a man converted through an experience of such miraculous cure indicates that the pattern is traditional:

I have been in the valley of the shadow of death and my restoration to life and health is thought by many to be little short of a miracle. Having been crippled for over thirty years by spinal and sciatic rheumatism, I had no hope of ever recovering, and was resigned to the Lord's will. In January I fell on the ice, resulting in concussion of the spine and fracture of the hip bone, breaking the two principal bones. For more than three months I was unable to move a finger. Friends sent me three of the best surgeons they could find and all three agreed that it was useless even to prescribe for me, that recovery was impossible. Finally when all looked for me to die at any moment, a poor old colored friend (a Witness), a Christian woman, said to me, "You never tried Doctor Jesus. He can cure you. Now pray with me to rejoice, for we will be heard." So we prayed and soon I noticed an improvement. Today I am not only better in health, but I can walk better than in thirty years, and all traces of my old infirmity are gone. . . .

While I lay helpless I thought of how I would try to lead others to the light. I had often thought to devote my time and labor to the Lord and his kingdom work and am longing to do so now if it is his will.[30]

Such cures are seldom claimed by the Witnesses today, although it is not denied that they do take place as a result of true belief. Present-day Witnesses are so impressed with the idea of the end of the age that they are unable to see and unwilling to grant importance to any other aspect of religion. A few believe that to summon a doctor is evidence of a "superstitious" nature, and therefore refuse medical attention when they are ill, confident that "if Jehovah God wants me to be well, he will keep me so." The majority, however, accept medical services.

The Witnesses of the larger cities attend motion picture theaters; seldom do they attend plays. The ideal Witness, however, does not visit motion picture houses too often, since to do so would be to deprive the service work of an adequate share of his spare time. Sometimes it is not

[29] *Ibid.*, Aug., 1896. [30] *Ibid.*, Jan., 1897.

easy for a Witness to decide how many movies he may attend. Once when I was returning from a Witness court trial with two Pioneers, who were sisters, one expressed an inclination for a movie while the other said that she felt that they had been attending too many. After discussing the matter, the first sister decided that she would not be "robbing the Lord of his time" if she went, but the other felt duty-bound to begin her service work as quickly as possible.

In the smaller towns, however, and in the rural areas, there are Witnesses who hold that attending a motion picture theater is a sign of being under the control of Satan. Rural Witnesses have told me that they think the motion picture theaters are bait used by the Devil to ensnare "the Lord's people." The theaters are considered by these Witnesses to be part of "Satan's organization," distracting people from their daily hardships and responsibilities and tending to replace God by offering a substitute solace for their cares.

Rural and city Witnesses are agreed upon several practices. One has to do with eating. The problem of special food habits was considered early in the movement's history and the decision was made by Mr. Russell that the group should not concern itself over such matters, that everyone was entitled to eat what he chose. This seems to have been a concession to Jewish Witnesses who felt obligated to observe their dietary regulations even after conversion. In recent years this early decision was forgotten by many, and the question arose again. To meet it, Mr. Rutherford declared in 1939 that all food is "religiously clean," and added, "I see no reason why anyone should hold that ham and bacon are unclean." [31] Various Jewish Witnesses who have come from orthodox backgrounds have told me that they no longer observe the dietary laws of their former religion; their association with the Witnesses has liberated them.

Although animals may be slaughtered for food, the late leader of the Jehovah's Witnesses specifically enjoined his followers not to kill them for sport. Mr. Rutherford was adamant upon this point, declaring that "no one is justified to hunt animals or fowl for sport, thrills or adventure." [32] Those who do so, he characterized as follows:

The indisputable facts show that a class of men who indulge in hunting wild beasts and fowls merely for the thrill and selfish pleasure derived therefrom are also the men who indulge and delight in military training and the prosecution of wars and who advocate wars, and also that to a large degree they are

[31] *Ibid.*, Feb., 1939.　　　　　　　　　[32] Rutherford, *Salvation*, p. 282.

religionists, given over to formalism and to the praise and adulation of men, all of which is done in direct opposition to and in defiance of God's law, and which therefore is sin.[33]

The injunction has caused some dissatisfaction among Witnesses who, prior to their conversion, had liked to hunt. There is some dispute among rural Witnesses as to whether they may kill rabbits for food and also to protect their crops.

The injunction against killing animals arises from basic factors dissimilar to those of many regions of India where belief in the transmigration of souls is prevalent. The Witnesses believe simply that Jehovah has commanded in the Bible that men should not kill animals except for food, and that animals, like men, are a creation of Jehovah and as such have significance in the divine plan.

The Witnesses are not agreed as to the desirable ethical consequences of conversion. A few of them look upon their conversion as the acceptance of new beliefs about God, the Bible, the course of history, and so on. A Michigan Witness wrote: "I had always thought that we had to develop a character, but now I know what is the principle thing, knowledge." [34] On the other hand, many Witnesses interpret their conversion largely in terms of conduct. To them, conversion means awakening to a new set of values to which they had previously been "blinded." They become dissatisfied if their conversion does not bring them greater desire to attain pure and clean lives. Often they are aware of specific moral gains: "I feel that the Lord is leading me; that I have more patience now than hitherto—which I greatly needed, and for which I often prayed." [35]

In still other cases the experience creates a desire to renounce person and possessions completely and to enter into the work:

I am ready and willing to leave all, earthly friendships, social ties, church-parish, ministerial office, salary, and even my own brothers and sisters and parents if necessary. Yes, I solemnly can say, I am willing to give myself with all that I am, and have, and shall be, to the ministry of this blessed truth, as a bond-servant of God and of the Lord Jesus Christ, knowing that the time is short.[36]

This minister of the Midwest illustrates a common form of self-renunciation among Witnesses. When a number of such devotees com-

---

[33] *Ibid.*, pp. 286–287.

[34] *Watch Tower*, Sept., 1926.

[35] *Ibid.*, Nov., 1892.

[36] *Ibid.*, Dec., 1898.

prise a Company, the effect upon unbelievers is electrifying. In one such case, even the visiting zone servant was impressed: "I was especially pleased with the brethren at Shoal Lake [Minnesota], on account of the plain improvement in their characters." [37]

The literature records many conversions of prisoners which have issued in definite moral changes. The Society is willing to send its literature free to inmates of penal institutions who ask for it. In this way prisoners have come to know the movement well, and some have been converted by the literature alone. The resolve of one converted prisoner is as follows:

However unfavorable my early surroundings, and however evil my early associations, I think I have cause for thankfulness that I have at last reached a point where I can see the right way ahead, and turn my back on the dark and wretched past. I am determined to pursue that way for the remainder of my life. I have been five years in this place, and have still three years and three months to serve.[38]

Conversion aids some Witnesses in solving their problems by the simple expedient of dismissing personal responsibilities and depending upon Jehovah to work them out. Frequently the problems are less ethical than economic: "Before we received the truth, I would lie awake 'till two or three o'clock in the morning trying to figure how to save this property. Now I go to bed, say the Lord's prayer, and in a few moments I am asleep." [39]

Sometimes conversion creates an increased sensitivity to moral problems. A typical case of the kind is worthy of extended review here because it demonstrates the attitude both of the individual and of the Society toward such problems. The person is a Witness from a small town in Pennsylvania:

Dear Brother: Last Sunday at our meeting we had a lesson from Romans 12:1 and among many thoughts brought out in such a prolific subject were some on the use we make of our consecrated time. I am engaged in the grocery business; but the conditions of trade in general demands almost "eternal vigilance" at the present time.

The question which has presented itself to me many times is: Should I, as one of the consecrated, put forth such efforts to make and maintain custom as is now necessary to do? I issue weekly price-lists, many times offering goods at less than cost for baits, and I give away many "gifts" with more profitable

[37] *Ibid.*, July, 1896.   [38] *Ibid.*, March, 1888.   [39] *Ibid.*, Aug., 1935.

goods; not of preference to that sort of dealing, but because all of my competitors are doing the same thing, and to maintain my trade and living, as I am not wealthy, I am compelled to follow suit.

Another objectionable feature about that kind of method is that it squeezes my weaker brother in the same line of business. I am acquainted with many of them; some are widows trying to make an honest living by selling goods; but I am compelled to throw all of my better feelings to the wind and "wade in," no matter whom it injures. This is a sad confession for one who is bidding for the position of assisting our Lord in the lifting of mankind out of the chasm of selfishness from which they must be saved in the age which we believe to be close at hand. I am not trying to get you to justify my action in this matter, but desire your opinion as to the advisable course of God's professed children engaged in business during the present time, when it is a case of the big fish eating the smaller ones.[40]

In reply, Russell told the conscience-stricken Witness that his problem was representative of many which confront true believers. The Witness was advised not to worry about the plight of poor widows caught in business competition, because such conditions are to be expected and are even intended in the course of human progress:

"Temporarily some poor widows or worthy ones may suffer through mental, physical or financial inability to keep up with the new order of things. And even these, if they take a broad, benevolent view of the situation, may rejoice in the public welfare, even though it enforces an unfavorable change in their own affairs."

Widows and "weaker" business people should look only toward that future order of society in which all such injustices would be eliminated. However, "only those who have the 'new Nature' and its love can be expected to view things unselfishly." The reply to the inquiring store-owner from Pennsylvania continued:

Our advice is that you keep a sharp outlook and if you see some other branch of business less beset with competition, and therefore more favorable, make a change. If not, or until you find a more favorable business, or more favorable conditions, we advise you to continue where you are and MODIFY your course to some extent; i. e., divide matters as evenly as you can between the three conflicting interests—your own, your competitors', and your patrons' or neighbors' interests. If your business is meeting expenses and affording a reasonable profit, endeavor to keep it there, but do not push it in the endeavor to become

[40] Russell, *Studies in the Scriptures,* IV, 522–525.

"Rich," for "they that WILL to be rich fall into temptation and a snare." We should avoid all dishonorable competition or meanness toward competitors, and any misrepresentation of goods to customers. Justice and honesty must be carefully guarded at ANY COST; then add all the moderation in favor of your competitor that love may suggest and that circumstances permit.[41]

Sometimes the conversion experience causes remorse over injustices committed in the past. A Witness in England testified:

At a meeting of Witnesses, a sister quoted the words of our Lord, "Owe no man anything," and said that if any had stolen anything previous to their conversion they should replace it. I had never heard of this before, and was greatly disturbed. I robbed my father many times, and many others. I was in London at the time, and wrote immediately and told my father of my misdeeds. He was aware of them to a certain extent. I knew not the full amount of them myself; as it was over a series of years, but I confessed as fully as I knew how, and he very kindly answered that whatever I had robbed him of he freely forgave me, and ever since I think he has looked upon me as rather weak in the mind. I went to some and repaid and wrote to others. Among others was the Metropolitan Street Railroad Company of Boston. I was a conductor of their cars for ten months, and defrauded them of a considerable amount; I know not how much. . . . I wrote acknowledging my fault to the Metropolitan Street Railroad Company in Boston saying that although I had not the means then should I ever have it I would send such a sum as would assuredly cover all my theft. I cried to the Lord to teach me his way and equipped thus I enquired of all who I thought could help me, and although many gave their opinion, some one way and some another, yet none offered me evidence to convince me from the Scriptures, and that is my present difficulty.[42]

The writer was counseled not to repay any more of the money he had taken in earlier life, because since his conversion his "old self" had "died," and he was now living "as though you ACTUALLY were dead." Because the difference between a person who is a believer and one who is not is so great and unbridgeable, the believer is in no sense responsible either technically or morally for his actions before a conversion. This doctrine brings relief to many Witnesses who before conversion had formed responsibilities including those of marriage.

Often the experience of conversion brings Witnesses to doubt the necessity of regular employment. Believing that Jehovah has decreed

[41] *Ibid.*   [42] *Watch Tower*, Oct., 1885.

the end of the age and that the event is to occur "very soon," many Witnesses feel that they should not continue in regular employment but should drop everything and go out to preach the acceptable day of the Lord. As one Witness put it: "How I long to be relieved of certain business responsibilities encumbered during these past 1260 days." [43] Regular employment seems almost an unbearable burden to most Witnesses; its interests conflict with their new status as believers: "Has a man who has consecrated himself to his Father's business any right to engage in the ordinary duties of life? Can he do so and fulfill his baptismal vow?" [44] The answer to such a question usually "hedges" the chief concern of the inquirer, who is told that he must not dismiss his earthly responsibilities, but at the same time he must not permit them to interfere with his heavenly ones. In interpreting this kind of answer, Witnesses have always disagreed. Some have stopped work because they found it did distract them from the new goal:

Perhaps it may interest you to know something of MY PLANS for the future. I HAVE NONE. I have closed up my business; and as a believer I have made full surrender to the Master. My only desire is to be led by him, and that I might devote the remainder of my time for this age, as well as for the age to come, in his service.[45]

Very often they volunteer as Pioneers. A Witness from Texas thus offered his services:

Although not a very old man, yet I have become convinced that I don't want any longer to be an active practitioner of my profession as a lawyer, for the reason that I want to wholly sever my relations with any and all worldly organizations, so that I will not have anything to divide my loyalty toward the coming kingdom.[46]

Almost all of the Witnesses are agreed that full-time service for the organization is the best of all possible jobs. Some speak of it as "my next job."

The institution of marriage is considered in a special light. On the whole, marriage among Witnesses is nowadays officially discouraged. Several reasons are given for this attitude. Marriages in this life take

[43] *Ibid.*, June, 1925.   [44] *Ibid.*, March, 1895.
[45] *Ibid.*, May, 1885. A manufacturer of alcoholic beverages reported that upon conversion, "I poured to waste all of my liquors and renounced the Roman Catholic Church." *Ibid.*, Jan., 1889.
[46] *Ibid.*, Dec., 1935.

place in an evil, Satan-controlled world; but if the believers would only wait a short time, the marriage could be consummated in the God-established world. Moreover, children born of present-day marriages will be judged by God according to the standards of this age, which means that they must be true believers in order to be saved. Children brought into this world are imperfect, subject to death, whereas, those born in the millennium will be physically perfect and will not suffer death. Then too, the organization has found from experience that marriage tends to decrease the zeal of Witnesses, for as soon as couples establish homes they are distracted from their primary task of saving the world, and, finding their major satisfaction at home, often neglect the Witness work or even quit the movement.

Several opinions prevail among Witnesses as to the value of marriage in the millennium. Some feel that it will be continued in the coming perfect world simply because Jehovah ordained it in the past as a divine institution, and anything God himself has created must be good and must be permanent. These believe that Witnesses now married will remain in that state after the end of the age; that they will be able to have children, and will have the joy of seeing them free from all harm, sickness, or any evil thing. To Witnesses who find themselves unable in this life to have the children they long for, this is a comforting thought.

Others believe that marriage will disappear after the inception of "the new world order." To them, the basis for marriage is not communion of like-minded spirits, but merely lust. The sexual relation is low in their scale of values, and will therefore not be carried over into the purity of the new age. That sexual relations often distract the Witnesses from their tasks, the majority of them agree. Moreover, women are "the root of all evil." The Witnesses believe that God does not favor "women's rights," for if he did he would have said so in the Bible. Instead, he pictures woman as a detriment to the finest spiritual development of man. The Witnesses often quote the story of Adam and Eve to show that a woman was the primary cause of the downfall of the human race; the wiles of the Devil in the Edenic tale were successfully met until the woman fell and in turn bewitched the man. To prove that women are much "weaker" than men, the story of Lot's wife is a favorite.

Witnesses consider it unnecessary to secure the services of licensed civil or religious authorities for a marriage ceremony. Mr. Rutherford loudly protested against the religious authorities especially, who, he felt, perform marriage ceremonies without the authorization of Jehovah and purely for monetary reasons. The civil authorities also represent a part of "Satan's organization"; marriages performed by them are not recognized by Jehovah. Mr. Rutherford approved of the Old Testament marriage of Isaac and Rebekah [47] at which no "third party" was present, for the good reason that God had ordained the marriage and was watching over the couple. In another passage, Mr. Rutherford compared human marriage to that of the church to Christ, capitalizing upon a simile of the New Testament.[48] In the marriage of the church to Christ, Mr. Rutherford explained, there also was no "third party" except God.[49] This doctrine was formulated soon after Mr. Rutherford came into the Society's leadership. It was received by many of the Witnesses as "communistic," "heretical," and so on. Some, being naturally conservative in such matters, thought it could have been formulated only by Satan, and promptly left the organization. To others, however, the doctrine had definite appeal. Still others wrote to the Society's leader and asked for further Scriptural proof. As a result, *The Watch Tower* carried many articles on marriage, all of which tried to placate the dissenters and at the same time to maintain Rutherford's original position on the doctrine.

Although, in general, the Witnesses were not denied the privilege of marrying, to those of the "Jonadab class" specific injunctions were issued against it:

Those Jonadabs who now contemplate marriage, it would seem, would do better if they waited a few years, until the fiery storm of Armageddon is gone, and then to enter into the marital relationship and enjoy the blessings of participating in filling the earth with righteous and perfect children. . . . What should the Jonadabs do now? They should devote themselves to the kingdom interests wholly.[50]

Some present-day Witnesses do marry. Those of more conservative bent usually seek a civil or religious service, but this concession to "worldliness" is not viewed with favor by their more zealous brethren. More often the civil authorities are called upon than the religious, because of the firm prejudice against the latter. A few Witnesses have married without the aid of either. In that case a close friend is usually asked to lead a sort of marriage service, different in some ways from that of

[47] Genesis 24: 58, 61–67.   [48] Matthew 25: 6, 7, 10.
[49] Rutherford, *Marriage*, pp. 36, 43.
[50] Rutherford, *Face the Facts*, pp. 50–51. See p. 60, above.

the churches. No special garb is worn and there is no feasting. After the ceremony, the couple sometimes recall with comfort the card which Witnesses carry entitling them to be called "ministers." Not many of these marriages have been entered upon, and they generally take place among those who are especially strong in the faith. What happens to such marriages can only be a matter of conjecture, as so far no scientific survey of them is possible.

One of the surest proofs of true faith, according to many Witnesses, is family strife. Generally they pride themselves upon difficulties which follow from religious differences within the family and often quote the words of Jesus to the effect that for the truth a Christian may have to forsake even his own family. In many cases the wife or the husband is a Witness but the other is not. If the Witness refuses to comply with his or her marriage obligations and shuns his mate as "belonging to the Devil," separation frequently results. Witnesses believe that true disciples should not marry out of "the truth," and hold intermarriage between believers and unbelievers in aversion. They are told that such marriages do not have the approval of Jehovah and only invite disruption. Seldom does family strife lead to divorce, however, because the movement is strictly opposed to it. Although no exact figures can be obtained as yet, I have the impression that the number of separations among the Witnesses is unusually high compared to those of other religious groups.

One of the first obligations of a newly converted Witness is to testify to his own family about his experiences. In the case of young people who have been converted, this testimony is not always received by their parents with great joy. Quite often a son or daughter leaves the family because the parents have been unable to accept the new-found faith. In these cases, the youths look upon their parents as "less than human" and quote with relish such Bible verses as "When my parents forsake me, then will the Lord take me up," and "Who is my father or my mother?" [51] I have been led to believe that the number of these cases is unusually high among the Witnesses.

Receiving "the truth" has many effects upon marriage and the family. One woman described her devotion to the cause, saying, in regard to her children, that she would "give up not only my church, but my loved ones

[51] Psalm 27:10; Matthew 12:48.

also." [52] But it has also happened within the history of the movement that coming into "the truth" has increased parental love and care:

I have taken a new interest in my boys. I have come to realize that they are not my own boys, but the Lord's; bought and owned by him, and perhaps consecrated to him, they always say they are; so I am trying to be more careful of them, and I feel free to admire them as never before. I can see what precious little souls they are, and how all their intentions are for righteousness. It is pleasing to notice that they are perfectly truthful, and always scrupulously honest in all business matters. [53]

What mother would not enjoy being able to say such things about her children; and what son would not like to be so trusted!

Neglect of wives seems to be another characteristic of the marital relations of Witnesses. Often husband and wife engage in service work in different parts of a town. The work is so demanding that most of the free time of the Witnesses is taken up with it; thus, husband and wife are commonly unable to share their experiences, except for an occasional "report" on their activities at the end of a tiring day. If there are children in the family, quite often the wife is forced to stay at home while the husband attends the Witness meetings and carries on "the Lord's work." This seems perfectly proper to some, but others consider it a neglect of marital obligations:

I am sorry, very sorry to say it, but many times I have found on close acquaintance with the brethren in the truth, men who professed full consecration, that they neglected their wives so very bad relative to the truth. Seemingly anxious to spread the truth amongst their friends, and neighbors, yet they make no provision for their wives so that they could attend the meetings and would even talk before their families in such a way as to leave the impression that maybe the truth was not for their wives and children. [54]

The movement has never approved of divorce, except on "New Testament grounds." This is taken to mean that no Witness should seek a divorce except for adultery, and as we have noted, most of those who are separated from their spouses refuse to seek divorce. The fact that the founder was divorced has always been a stumbling block to some Witnesses. It has also provided a precedent for the permissibility of alimony. Mr. Rutherford testified to the fact that he and four other prominent

[52] *Watch Tower*, Aug., 1904.   [53] *Ibid.*, June, 1896.   [54] *Ibid.*, Dec., 1907.

Witnesses grouped together in 1909 to raise "$10,000 which they paid to Mrs. Russell for back alimony. From 1909 until the time of the death of Mr. Russell, these men paid Mrs. Russell $100. a month out of their own funds." [55] How they were able to pay such large sums of money when they were ostensibly working for room, board, and a nominal allowance per month, has never been made clear.

On the whole the Witnesses follow in sex matters the mores of their local communities. But a large percentage of cases evidencing marital disorganization can be found among them. In rural areas sex is generally a matter of secrecy and a puritanical profession of chastity. In cities, however, conduct may be different.

While the Witness attitude toward sex appears to the observer to be less formal than among some other groups, there is also another side to the story. Charges of sexual laxity are likely to be brought against any new religious or social sect that opposes certain commonly held values. In the period of the Enlightenment, one of the most effective weapons of the intellectuals against the power and prestige of the clergy was this charge. In recent years, before the present war, communistic Russia was gravely criticized because of its novel attitude toward marriage and the family. Now it is popular to point to the sexual perversions of Mr. Adolf Hitler. In view of this context, similar criticism of the Witnesses—which has recently become fairly common—cannot be accepted as totally unbiased. But, while recognizing that some of it may be unfair, the movement nevertheless does seem to provide more than ordinary opportunities for sexual laxity.

Not much attention is given to children. Although the latest work published by the Society is entitled *Children,* it was not written for them. However, that even the title of a book should be devoted to them seems to signify that the organization is becoming more conscious of youth in terms of potential membership. The Witnesses have been instructed not to seek to convert children of unbelievers, because this practice leads to strife in the homes and often increases parental resistance toward the movement. They do, however, try to convert their own children. [56] Many are proud of the fact that their children study the Bible and the writings of Mr. Rutherford and show the impress of what they have heard and read. Some of the youngsters with whom I have spoken have been quite adept in the use of Witness clichés. Their problems indicate

[55] *Ibid.,* Feb., 1917.   [56] Rutherford, *Face the Facts,* p. 48.

the extent of their indoctrination. They do not worry about the existence and character of Santa Claus or whether Jack Frost really paints the trees with ice in the winter time; they are concerned with vague theological conceptions, such as is disclosed by the following:

I am a young girl aged fourteen years, and have been a publisher for Jehovah for four years. I was told the other day by a brother that I am not a Christian. Would you please give me two Scriptures to prove I am not; and if not a Christian, what can I say if someone asks me at a door what I am? [57]

When the children of Witnesses do not accept the instruction of their parents, serious problems are created; the parents are inclined to regard those who refuse as "dupes of Satan" and may show marked favoritism toward those of their children who accept "the truth." One Witness told me that her son was "an enemy just as sure as any unbeliever." Another Pioneer Witness was sorely distressed because her daughter not only refused to accept "the truth," but was engaged to marry a Roman Catholic boy. This family split tended to lower the mother's prestige among the Witnesses. The mother constantly besought her daughter, even in public meetings, to become a Witness. The girl usually replied that she could not "see" all of the teachings of the movement. The mother excused her daughter's refusal on the grounds that she "loved the world too much."

There is little in the organization of the present Society and its local Companies which ministers especially to the religious needs of Witness children. The movement has always hated Sunday Schools, calling them "a thing of the past" and "a tool of the Devil." Sunday Schools are criticized because they remove parental responsibility for religious instruction in the home and because they are simply "advance-agents" of a church in getting new members.[58] The lesson materials which Sunday Schools use, chiefly the International Sunday School Lessons, are considered to be prejudiced evilly against the only true interpretation of the Word of God.[59] From the beginning of the movement, the mention of "Sunday School" has been met with derisive laughter. In one Company meeting, when the leader had "stumped" the group with a question, he suggested that what they probably needed was a "Sunday School." This remark was sufficient to chide them into a more diligent study of *The Watch Tower.*

[57] *Watch Tower*, Oct., 1937.   [58] Russell, *Studies in the Scriptures*, III, 144.
[59] *Ibid.*, pp. 142–144.

Young People's Societies are also criticized by the Witnesses, who have nothing like them for their own children. The various youth societies, formed generally under church supervision, are condemned as being too superficial in their approach to the Bible and to religious problems as such. The Witnesses point out that many of these societies seldom consider for discussion subjects of a biblical nature, but are chiefly interested in holding parties—"they care more for dancing than for the Word of God." [60] Moreover, young people's societies, like Sunday Schools, are instruments of the churches for the extension of membership. In England, however, Witnesses grouped themselves together in 1929 to form the Junior Bible Students Company which was composed of child Witnesses from all over England. This group held conventions and went about its affairs quite like the parent organization of English Witnesses (the International Bible Students Association). Recently, however, the children's group has not been functioning.

On first sight, the Jehovah's Witnesses seems to lack adequate formal means of instruction for its children, and the Witnesses openly admit this. But, upon closer examination, one may discover that preparation in the faith of their parents has not been neglected. In general, such instruction has been removed from the jurisdiction of the Society to that of the parents. Witnesses do, however, welcome children to their meetings, which prove to be substitutes for "the evil Sunday Schools." In Company meetings the children may take part in the answering of questions, and in house meetings they may inquire about the organization and its teachings. If they care to become Witnesses, they are received even as older people are, and placed in the service work. The Witnesses feel that child workers are particularly effective, since oftentimes they can obtain a hearing when grown-ups cannot.

From its beginning the movement has minimized the significance of formal education. For, is not the age coming to an end? Believing as they do, the Witnesses are inclined to derogate every distinction or means of gaining social prestige which is not based on that of "sainthood" as the Witnesses mean it. Everything else is "worldly" and of value only to those of "the world." The founder of the movement said of college education: "If every man were a college graduate conditions would be much worse than today. Education is not for the masses." [61] Mr. Russell held this position because he felt that education is founded on pride.

[60] *Watch Tower*, Aug., 1895.   [61] Russell, *Studies in the Scriptures*, IV, 450.

Those who attend college are simply seeking to increase their own importance through education. The Word of God opposes pride; education, therefore, tends to nullify its teachings (and, presumably, forbids the teaching of the Bible and of faith in God). According to Mr. Russell: "One of the greatest difficulties of present-day education, which leads to pride, arrogance, and discontent, is its lack of elementary wisdom." And if we ask what constitutes "elementary wisdom," we are told that it is "reverence of the Lord." [62] In cases where religion is taught in schools, especially in theological seminaries, the purpose primarily is to "inculcate the ideas of the so-called 'Systematic Theology' . . . and to fetter free thought." [63]

Mr. Russell and Mr. Rutherford were skillful propagandists, and were well grounded in a consistent program of theological instruction, yet neither claimed to be well educated. The noticeable absence of formal education among the Witnesses has been one of their chief claims to glory. Yet, at the turn of the last century the Society sought to create a system of instruction by mail which would raise the educational standards of its full-time workers. A Witness who passed a comprehensive theological examination received the degree (not legally conferred) of "Verbi Dei Minister" or V.D.M. as it was popularly known. He received a card on which was printed his name and his degree, signed by the president of the Society. But, about 1915 the Society discontinued this practice, because many outsiders came to consider those who possessed the degree as the officially constituted clergy of the organization. Moreover, the granting of special privileges to some Witnesses tended to engender jealousy among others less distinguished.

The Witnesses are thoroughly pessimistic about any form of "social uplift." They believe that it is wiser to reject the evil world and to concentrate upon saving individuals from it for the future, perfect world. This view was conceived first by Mr. Russell and was developed to its logical conclusion by Mr. Rutherford. Mr. Russell surveyed some of the grave social ills of his time—unemployment, war, divorce—and came to the conclusion that all of these problems are "corporately beyond human power to regulate." [64] Any attempt to improve the living conditions of men was considered "unscriptural and erroneous." [65] He argued that only two possibilities were open to religiously minded people (like

---

[62] *Ibid.*, p. 639. Cf. Proverbs 1:7; 9:10.
[63] *Ibid.*, p. 64.   [64] *Ibid.*, p. 381.   [65] *Ibid.*, p. 172.

most doctrinaires he seldom found more than two alternatives). The first of these was: conversion of the whole world en masse to the basic principles of Jesus; the other, the direct intervention of superhuman power.[66] The Witnesses still agree that for them the only solution of world evil is the second. The Witness lives in two worlds; he seeks, however, to live only in one. The world in which he would like to live is more compellingly attractive than the one in which he actually finds himself. His conception of the "kingdom" at the end of history is not that of William Blake, for example, who dreamed of establishing God's kingdom upon "England's green and pleasant land." The Witness kingdom is earthly only in the sense that it supposedly will be established here on this planet and not on any other. The future society has no connection with or resemblance to that of the present. The Witnesses find it difficult to coöperate with national governments, for these are diametrically opposed to the one which will be established in the future. In a letter on the subject, one believer indicates the official attitude of the Society, which is that all governments are so wicked that the true believer simply cannot coöperate with them in any way:

How much we owe to those who of yore took up the sword, and fought for the rights of man; yet it seems now we must not do it. How I have longed since a youth to take up the sword and fight for the oppressed; but the teachings of your books are against such a course, and I am forced to admit that you are right.[67]

Thus, under the compulsion of an idea of an Utopian future, most Witnesses refuse to coöperate with any agency which seeks to ameliorate the ills of life.

[66] *Ibid.*, p. 311.   [67] *Watch Tower*, Jan., 1895.

The Witness as Believer

To the Witnesses the problem of belief is central. They assume their movement to be founded upon beliefs that are novel in the history of religions, and to a certain extent they are right. From a broader point of view, however, all their beliefs have appeared previously in one or more of the religions of the world, although naturally not in identical forms. Moreover, several of the other distinctive American forms of religious expression have also possessed beliefs similar not only in content but also in motivation.

Among some religious groups the problem of "right" belief is of secondary importance. This is true of the Liberal Protestants, who for many years have been more concerned with proper action, especially in the social area, than with proper beliefs in the theological realm. Upon being confronted with the very real problem of war, however, the Liberal Protestants reacted in several ways. To some, the rise of the present war brought the negation of essential Christianity and, at the same time, a betrothal of science with humanly conceived values for the attainment of a lasting, stable social order. To others, the present war brought about a reversal of their former position to such an extent that problems of belief became of prime importance, while social judgment and even social participation were relegated to the background.

The Jehovah's Witnesses stand in sharp contrast to such a group. They not only have a system of beliefs upon which they depend for solace and security, but they also consider the problem of belief as of paramount significance. Correct belief is to many Witnesses more important than improvement of character. Relations to men in the work-a-day world are secondary. Salvation does not depend upon any particular kind of defined moral conduct either before or after conversion, but depends simply upon acceptance of "the truth." "The truth" not only makes man free, it is the key which opens to him all mysteries and solves all problems. If one of the Witnesses has become discouraged or sick, the malady is not traced to a disturbance of the glands, wrong diet, or overwork, and the like, but to a relaxing of some doctrinal position. The cure is not medical but theological, for if his ideas can be straightened out to conform with those of the movement, then sickness or unhappiness will vanish.

The accent on religious understanding gained from books rather than from life itself does not generally make for a type of religious experience that is permanent and satisfying. The satisfactions derived from such a conception of religion at best are temporary and need constant bolstering by various techniques. The believer usually minimizes life experience and stresses the significance of book experience: "I could sit here for hours and write about all the wonderful things which I've learned during the past year about Jehovah and his Word." [1]

The belief system of the Jehovah's Witnesses is totalitarian. The theology does not attempt to make a partial inquiry into the nature of reality, but claims to have succeeded already in obtaining the final answer to all important religious problems. One of the delights of Witnesses is to state proudly that there is no question which they cannot answer successfully. Obviously, such a rigid acceptance of dogma precludes any of the spontaneity that comes from fresh, creative attempts at problem solving in the religious area. The beliefs laid down by Mr. Russell and developed and modified by Mr. Rutherford still remain unchanged for the most part. This immutability has an appeal to many who desire some point of stability in a mercurial world. Some Witnesses think that the fixity of their beliefs constitutes adequate proof of reliability. In 1931 one of the Witnesses said: "Away back in 1884 I made the resolution to stick to the Watch Tower Bible and Tract Society until, or unless, it would indisputably renounce the Ransom." [2] This characteristic has caused one conservative Protestant to describe the movement as "the bold system." [3] And such it is, for it claims to be the final and complete revelation of Jehovah.

This craving for completeness which characterizes many Witnesses is illustrated in a story told me by one of them. He said that when he was a youth his parents bought an expensive phonograph and a great number of records. Within the phonograph were record compartments. His parents, though lovers of music, were not lovers of system and therefore kept the records in any compartment and in any haphazard arrangement. For a time, he said, this did not disturb him, but gradually he came to see that the one thing that was lacking was a principle of order. Therefore, with typical Witness persistence, he set about classifying and arranging the records according to his own system of organization. He looked upon this as a great accomplishment.

[1] *Watch Tower*, March, 1932.   [2] *Ibid.*, April, 1931.
[3] Jan K. van Baalen, *Our Birthright*.

The acceptance of the theology of the movement is a matter of "all or none." That is to say, that no Witness can long remain in the fold with an eclectic attitude toward beliefs. He cannot choose part of the Lutheran creed and part of the Witness belief. He cannot say that he accepts certain tenets because they have been successfully proven to him, but that acceptance of other parts must await similar proof. He cannot voice Spinoza's sentiment of believing as much as reason allows; to do this would be one of the gravest sins known in the Society's scale of values. Immediately upon conversion, the neophyte declares himself in harmony with all the beliefs of the organization whether he understands them or not—and often he has not even heard of some of them. If a Witness is unable to "see" a particular belief which the organization cherishes, he is taken aside by other Witnesses and persuaded that he has not made a complete surrender to the will of Jehovah, or that Satan has managed to creep into his life. The others pray that he may cast out Satan and accept the true belief. The effects of this procedure are obvious. The doubter feels that his moral integrity is under suspicion and the matter is oftentimes solved upon another basis than that of reasonable belief.

The whole movement has been built on authoritarian methods. This point cannot be overstressed. There has been only one real leader since the death of Russell. This was Rutherford, and his word was law. What he declared to be true, humble Witnesses the world round believed to be true, forgetting the words of the leader himself: "It is entirely unsafe for the people to rely upon the words and doctrines of imperfect men." [4] For years hyperorthodox Witnesses have lived in an unquestioning devotion to their leader. They do not think until they have heard an official declaration. They do not express their views; they repeat their leader's views as a phonograph repeats the first impression of a record. One Pioneer Witness wrote to Mr. Rutherford: "I have always been slow to challenge anything that has been sent out from the Society's headquarters, and I trust that it will ever be the same." [5] Deviations from the Rutherford gospel are reported quickly to the central organization. The case of the schismatic Mr. Salter, the Society's former representative for the whole of Canada, reveals an espionage almost parallel to the secret spy systems of Europe. When heresy is reported to the central organization the heretic is brought before a Company council and is usually immediately isolated from other Witnesses. In the case of Salter,

---

[4] Rutherford, *Prophets Foretell Redemption*, p. 35.   [5] *Watch Tower*, Feb., 1929.

the organization sent out word by letter and later through the official magazines that Salter was dismissed and that all true believers who valued their connection with the organization should have nothing to do with him.[6] In the case of Moyle, the former legal advisor, the action was the same.

There are some Witnesses, however, who think that the theology of the organization is not true in all aspects, but who are willing to coöperate with the movement to the extent that they feel able. One such person wrote to Mr. Rutherford:

Although I might not be able to see eye to eye with you in all of the non-essential points—and that is not at all necessary—I am with you on all of the doctrinal points and am certainly in harmony with the work that you are doing; it is the Lord's work.[7]

The typical reaction to such an offer of coöperation is that Jehovah's Witnesses does not need the help of these partial believers, for God alone is its strength. The Society advises such writers to continue to work upon the "non-essentials" until they feel in complete accord with the movement, and only then to begin the Witness work. Those Witnesses whose religion, like that of Rabelais, is a great "Perhaps" are very few indeed.

This arrogant spirit of the organization is derived in part from its conception of divine mission. The Witnesses firmly believe that they, and only they, represent the will of God for men on earth at this time. Claiming this, they also believe that they do not need the aid of any person or organization in the attainment of their goals. Once in speaking with Mr. Arthur Gaux, a member of the Board of Directors, I reminded him that my investigations were not viewed adversely by the American Civil Liberties Union and by others who were interested in the Witness movement. I also reminded him that the American Civil Liberties Union had voluntarily aided the Society on many occasions in their legal problems. Mr. Gaux promptly told me in a rather curt way that the Society did not "care a hoot" about the American Civil Liberties Union or any other organization. He said that if the Union cared to assist the Society it could, but that the Society did not recognize any obligation toward it. The Union, said Mr. Gaux, was not led by Jehovah and unfortunately did not have "the truth."

Between total belief and unbelief there is no gap deep or impassable

[6] *Ibid.*, April, 1937.   [7] *Ibid.*, Aug., 1920.

enough to restrain the true believer. As a poet has put it: "Believing hath a core of unbelieving." [8] Many Witnesses have been converted from total disbelief to the acceptance of the full Witness theology. The following is a typical statement:

Thirty years ago I rejoiced in the knowledge of the truth to learn that Jehovah was NOT. Now I rejoice to know that he IS. True the negative force was pleasing and then satisfying because our capacity was small. Now a positive force more than satisfies our most extravagant desires. [9]

Thus, to many Witnesses there is little difference in terms of motivation between total unbelief and total belief. Both attitudes of mind generally include only points of view and data favorable to themselves and exclude all else. Both attitudes are equally satisfying to those who hold them. To many persons the content of the total belief is unimportant: the only significant factors are whether or not the belief is complete, systematic, denying all opponents, and so on. In this sense the "atheism" from which many of the Witnesses claim deliverance was about the same sort of religious experience for them as their new belief, for both entail structurally the same psychological states of love, antagonism, security, and contentment.

The will to believe is so great among Witnesses that the content of belief becomes incidental. This attitude toward religious experience is typical among the naïve; and such, as a whole, are the Witnesses, whose literal-mindedness and unsophistication become almost ludicrous to minds unsympathetic to their cause. For example, one person was converted as a result of a notice which was inserted by him in two Chicago newspapers and which read as follows:

PERSONAL NOTICE

Correspondence wanted from anyone who is a candidate for absolute and abstract truth. Address, Box 142, ———, Illinois. [10]

The advertiser received literature from many groups claiming the key to eternal truth; among them was the Jehovah's Witnesses, to which he was finally converted. This man did not believe that "truth" is like corn which the farmer scatters to chickens—plural, segmentized. He thought of "truth" as a sugar cube which he could put into his drink—single,

---

[8] Robert W. Buchanan, *Complete Poetical Works* (London, 1901), I, 280: "Songs of Seeking," Canto XII.

[9] *Watch Tower*, March, 1931.   [10] *Ibid.*, Sept., 1897.

dispersible. He did not expect to search and find "truth" at the cost of "blood, sweat, and tears"; he expected it to come packed and ready for use. He would not agree with Montaigne that we are born only to seek after the truth perpetually.

The Witnesses who engage in field service usually find that their message appeals to the artless almost immediately upon presentation. "Wise" people do not respond as quickly, so Mr. J. B. Adamson, one of the first Witness Pioneers, testifies: "I avoid those wise men who know it all, whose creed is all in all for them, and go to those really hungry, among whom I find Christ's most precious people, and also many infidels." [11]

The character of the Witnesses' thinking is also revealed by the nature of their problems. Seldom have I found a Witness who was involved with a practical, experiential problem of religion. Most often the Witnesses are worried about theoretical, lifeless problems of religion, such as whether Jehovah spoke Hebrew or not, whether, to God, the angels are "higher" beings than man, whether the age will come to an end this year or next, etc. These matters are seemingly significant to many Witnesses, but to the outsider they reveal the paucity of real life-imbued religious experience. One of the Witnesses wrote to the Society's leader about a problem which to him was of great importance: "I hope and believe that I am one of the consecrated people, but do not know what member of the body I am. As I have no special gift as yet developed, I must be one of the feet members." [12] This, then, is the type of problem which bothers the Witnesses.

The attitude of the Witnesses toward the source of evil is also indicative of their general frame of mind. Many Witnesses believe that all of the wickedness ever committed has been committed by Satan. Men are not responsible for their wrongdoings, because Satan, the brilliant one, enters the minds of human beings and enforces his wickedness through them. Evil does not result from "a general feeling of evil" in the world; it is not regarded as an impersonal principle; it is not instigated by man. The belief in Satan is so real that Luther's act of throwing an ink bottle at the devil is used by a few Witnesses as proof to Protestants of the personal existence of evil. We have encountered one example of this attitude in the story of the ouija board. Similar cases that involve actual mental disturbances often go unrecognized:

[11] *Ibid.*, Nov., 1881.   [12] *Ibid.*, Sept., 1882.

They [several Witnesses] went to supper and Brother J. was asked to invoke the blessing. He had no more than finished when he jumped from the table and began to bounce over the room and scatter the furniture and to talk in an unknown language. This lasted about two minutes, and then it left him. He said, "Isn't it awful? They are trying to break down the truth." All suggested that they pray and did so, Brother J. joining in. But he broke right out again.

When he is rational he says that it is the fallen angels; but his people think he is crazy. He warned his wife against the evil spirits and said that they were very cunning and he could not resist doing the things they told him to do. He remembers all that he has done, but is in a stupor much of the time.[13]

The Witnesses have so intense a belief in the miraculous that many are willing to give their lives for it. They do not expect anything to come about through a gradual evolution. Results must come quickly or not at all. The world is evil and the efforts of humble men working together cannot better it. God must bring the new world if any is to be brought, and he will bring it suddenly and completely. The tremendous complexity of the present international struggle is passed off by the Witnesses as being incidental to a greater conflict in the heavens, where Satan is battling with God for supremacy.

The Witnesses display their naïveté in the political realm by not taking evil men like Hitler seriously. Before America entered the war, I discussed the problem of defeating Hitlerite Germany with a group of Witnesses. One of them told me not to worry about the plight of the world: if I would only believe in the Witness theology, all such problems would become of secondary importance. Another said that he could easily solve the international situation, if he had the opportunity and the power, by placing Hitler, Mussolini, Stalin, and Franco as a backfield in a football game against the professional New York Giants. He said that such a procedure would easily solve the problem of dictatorship. The other Witnesses, although smiling, agreed that that "would do the trick."

The beliefs of the Witnesses cannot be authenticated by knowledge gained in any area of study except the Bible. The leaders of the movement have always claimed that their theology cannot be "checked" upon by "secular" sources. Science, both in content and in method, is unable to contribute to an impartial appraisal because it "stands outside" the

[13] *Ibid.*, Nov., 1913.

revelation of Jehovah.[14] Nor can the study of history be called upon to verify the beliefs of Witnesses; in fact, it cannot even be used to substantiate the truth of the Bible: "Secular history is no standard by which to correct the supposed errors of the Bible. . . . We are not called upon to harmonize these [chronological data] with the tangled records of secular history." [15] The nature of proof is thereby limited to the statements of the Bible. No "secular" source is qualified to examine the Bible accurately—so-called "critics of the Bible" are of course classified as "secular."

The beliefs of the Witnesses are not related to experience. This is an advantage especially gloried in by some of the leaders of local groups. One such leader told me that he had several other religious affiliations before he came into the Witness movement. He said that the best feature of the movement to his mind was the fact that he did not have to try to harmonize his beliefs with his experience.

Very few Witnesses have any carefully reasoned explanation of the "other-worldliness" of their beliefs, which many compare to their childhood conceptions of life, declaring them more satisfying than any attempt to "see things as they are." To a large extent the Witness beliefs appear to be compensatory, appealing to those who are underprivileged both materially and emotionally and providing a means of escape from a not too-provident existence into a consistently pleasurable, victory-achieving realm. In the course of a discussion of reality, a Witness once argued with me about the "trickiness" of paintings. He said that art involves deception in the sense that it tries to express something which is actually unreal. But art is treasured by "wise" people because they feel it to be more expressive of reality than "reality" itself. Likewise, the beliefs of the Witnesses are unreal only in the sense that they are unrealized; if they were realized, they would be more beautiful and attractive than any present actuality. The Witness added that "the truth" comes from God and is revealed only by him; that, in Tertullian's phrase, "It is certain because it is impossible." This sort of discussion is not ordinarily possible among the Witnesses; in this instance my opponent, I was told by him and by others, had formerly been a professor at the University of Pennsylvania.

One of the compensatory beliefs in the theology of the Jehovah's Witnesses is that of "Destiny." Although this is more than slightly akin to

[14] Russell, *Studies in the Scriptures*, IV, 450.   [15] *Watch Tower*, July, 1923.

the views of Oswald Spengler, there is little probability that the leaders of the organization read such books as Spengler's *Decline of the West;* at any rate they never give credit to sources other than the Bible and God. The idea of Destiny was first suggested by Russell in the form of an elaborate chart which sought to demonstrate conclusively that the course of history was planful and would finally lead to the desire of every Witness heart—the theocracy. According to this view, the course of history has been controlled by Jehovah, who, having allowed the Devil to rule for some thousands of years, is about to resume power again.[16] To the Witnesses not only "hanging and wiving" go by Destiny, as Shakespeare thought, but all things.

All human history was divided by Russell into three stages: the world from the time of the creation to that of the flood; the present evil world, from the time of the flood to the final establishing of God's kingdom; and at last, the world to come.[17] According to the official teaching of the movement, each of these periods of human history, except the last, was marked by the progressive degeneration of mankind until finally Jehovah intervened.

The writings of both Russell and Rutherford contained two conflicting theories that have, in turn, been faithfully echoed by the Witnesses. The two leaders were agreed that the present world is becoming progressively more degenerate. At variance with this, both men occasionally intimated that the world may be undergoing "progress," though painfully. Periods of social calamity inclined them more strongly to the former attitude and periods of prosperity to the latter. Because the group has experienced more opposition than is welcome, the Witnesses have more consistently spoken of "the downward path of history":

For six thousand years the race has steadily pursued the broad, downward way. Only a few comparatively have tried to change their course and retrace their steps. In fact, to retrace all the steps, and reach the original perfection, has been impossible, though the effort of some to do so has been commendable, and not without results.[18]

Even Russell's pet socialism was rejected by the Witnesses because the course of history indicated to them that any such system would "soon be controlled by shrewd, selfish schemers." [19]

[16] Russell, *Studies in the Scriptures*, II, 42.
[17] *Ibid.*, I, 66.   [18] *Ibid.*, p. 206.   [19] *Ibid.*, IV, 487.

Part of the belief of the Witness in "the downward path of history" as determined by Destiny is that many individuals are basically "good," while all social institutions (except their own) are "evil." This doctrine can hardly come straight from Rousseau's *Emile* and other works, but it is quite like Rousseau's. The Witnesses believe that the individual is born into the world devoid of all evil because he is a child of God. But the surroundings of every human infant are evil, and as he grows older he appropriates more and more of these surroundings, until some have come to believe that the source of the evil lies in the very nature of the individual himself. The contradiction between this view and the concept of the Devil as the source of all evil does not worry the Witnesses.

The distinction between individuals and institutions is often applied to church members. I have asked Witnesses whether they condemn all members of other religious groups. They usually answer that the churches as institutions are controlled by Satan and are leading men away from Jehovah, but that there may be some fine individuals among them who are genuinely devoted to God. (This is in effect a restatement of the lines of *The Pirates of Penzance:* "Individually I love you all with affection unspeakable, but collectively, I look upon you with a disgust that amounts to absolute detestation.")

The individual is unable to break the strangle hold of evil institutions, and in this age must succumb to them. Nothing can stop "the downward path" of this age. The refinement of this century is viewed by the Witnesses as "a very thin veneer, easily peeled off." [20] Crime has increased to such an extent as to make the coming end of the age apparent to all.[21] The unjust gravitation of wealth into the hands of the few and at the expense of the many also makes the end certain.[22]

Another part of the conception of Destiny is the self-corruption of historical processes. The Witnesses reason that although several movements in the course of history have been started by outstandingly moral individuals, these movements have been consistently "overreached" by Satan until they have come to express the opposite of their original *raison d' être*. This is especially true of religions. For example, the Witnesses commonly believe that Christianity was begun by a noble, divine leader. In its early stages it truly expressed the will of God, and if its original purity had been maintained through the centuries, God would still be working through it. But, the pristine teachings of Jesus were

[20] *Ibid.*, p. 530.   [21] Rutherford, *The Kingdom*, p. 3.   [22] *Ibid.*

polluted early in the history of the religion by Paul, who, disregarding the will of God, weakened Christianity, systematizing and "churchifying" it until the resulting form was unsanctioned by God and was against the truest interests of man. In the opinion of the Witnesses the Roman Catholic Church may not have been founded by Jesus and St. Peter, but certainly it was by Satan and Paul. Thus, Paul is made the scapegoat for all the misinterpretations of the original Christian message. One of the surest signs to the Witnesses that the Roman Catholic Church corruptly follows "the religion of Paul" rather than "the religion of Jesus" is its historical affiliation with the political states of Europe and its present international, political character. The Witnesses agree with the pagan Lucretius that such religion tends to crush the finer aspects of man's development and is hateful in the eyes of all who truly "see." [23]

The Reformation also illustrates the principle of "overreaching"; it was inspired of God, but its divine usefulness was short-lived. "A bold and blessed stroke for liberty and the Bible was made in what is known as The Reformation. God raised up bold champions for his Word, among whom were Luther, Zwingli, Melancthon, Wycliffe, Knox, and others." [24] However, God's connection with the Reformation soon ceased, because the reformers forgot him, finding "the ways of men more pleasing." In the words of the Society's founder, the Reformation soon "was overcome by the spirit of the world." [25] Russell believed that Napoleon also had effected a reformation as notable as that of Luther when he succeeded in dominating Europe territorially at the expense of the pope. The results of Napoleon's reformation were overreached by Satan in the form of Mussolini who restored temporal power to the pope once more.

Since the Reformation, the original Christian message has been polluted further by both the Protestant as well as the Roman Catholic church. The Greek and Russian Orthodox churches follow in this tradition and are considered by the Witnesses simply as segments of the Roman Catholic Church. The corruption of the pure Christian message attained by Luther in the Reformation came about through the intervention of all churches in temporal matters. As Mr. Rutherford said: "No one will attempt to deny the fact that both of these great religious branches, Catholic and Protestant, have openly allied themselves with the political, commercial and military powers of the world." [26] At pres-

---

[23] Russell, *Studies in the Scriptures*, IV, 159–162.
[24] *Ibid.*, I, 23.   [25] *Ibid.*, IV, 160.   [26] Rutherford, *The Kingdom*, p. 12.

ent, Satan is overreaching every religious institution except that of the Jehovah's Witnesses. All present-day religion is a snare.[27]

Mr. Rutherford recognized only two forms of religion.[28] The first is the religion of all those who accept "the Lord's organization" or who are in "the truth." These are relatively few in number, but have had a history as long as that of the Bible (which was figured by an elaborate process to be about 6,000 years). Through this minority, Jehovah has sought to work out his will, which mainly consists in this age of simply telling every living person of "the truth."

The second kind of religion which Mr. Rutherford recognized consists of "world religions." Of all the world's living religions, aside from Judaism and Christianity, Mr. Rutherford seemed to know of only three: Islam, Buddhism, and Confucianism. Of these three systems he knew little beyond what is popular knowledge. He expressed, for example, the notion voiced by the sixteenth-century Robert Burton: "One religion is as true as another." Often he spoke of them as though they all were trying to dominate the world, while it is obvious that Confucianism does not have any missionary program other than that of Lin Yutang. These "world religions" were created by Satan, according to Mr. Rutherford, for the control through religion of the peoples of the earth.[29]

Taking his definition from facts, if such they may be called, with which most people are unfamiliar, Mr. Rutherford devised a definition of religion which makes it "the doing of anything contrary to the will of Jehovah." [30] The "will of Jehovah" is known only by the members of the Jehovah's Witnesses. In recent years the Witnesses have characterized the teachings of the churches as "religion" and the teachings of the Jehovah's Witnesses, "Christianity." "Religion" to the Witnesses is contrary to "Christianity" and has been organized by the Devil.[31]

Thus the course of human history largely has been downward; individuals are good while institutions are relatively insignificant in terms of their influence on the growth of personality; all historical processes tend

---

[27] Russell, *Studies in the Scriptures*, II, 279. "Religion as a snare" was first used as a catch phrase by Mr. Russell. It occurs in one of the volumes of *Studies in the Scriptures* in which religion is branded as a "delusive snare." Actually the phrase has a biblical background; it occurs, for example in I Timothy 6:9. In the same vein, Mr. Rutherford coined the phrase "religion as a racket."

[28] Rutherford, *Religions*, p. 12.

[29] Russell, *Studies in the Scriptures*, IV, 81.

[30] Olin Moyle, *Liberty to Preach*, p. 1.

[31] Rutherford, *Armageddon*, p. 12.

to become corrupt even as Christianity lost its original radiance. These are necessary and related parts of the general idea of Destiny as conceived by the Witnesses.

Although Destiny includes these factors, it can be trusted for the final triumph of good over evil. The many evils of our world will be crushed and a new world will be created in which evil can never again appear. The Witnesses trust this sacrosanct Destiny, believing that it will guarantee their "spiritual savings" against a "rainy day." Every event in history has its appointed time and cannot happen or fail to happen otherwise. Thus the "light" brought by the Jehovah's Witnesses is a part of this divine Destiny: "Why is it that such a light has not been revealed by some of the so-called wise and great before this? I suppose the time for it had not come." [32] Destiny will care for the Witnesses even in the minor, seemingly accidental, occurrences of life.[33] Although Destiny is often spoken of by the Witnesses as "the Lord," many times it is considered impersonally as though it were a compelling principle of cosmic order. At times it inspires the Witnesses to accelerated zeal in service and to mystical delights: "My soul is ravished with the indescribable excellency and magnitude of God's plan of salvation." [34] But, conversely, it may also lead to an appalling apathy in the face of evil. The Witnesses believe that there is nothing they can do to hasten or retard "the wave of the present." They voice the idea of Voltaire: "If you could disturb the destiny of a fly, there would be no reason to assume that you could be stopped in making the destiny of all other flies, of all the animals, of all men, of all nature; you would find yourself in the end more powerful than God." This amounts to the type of fatalism characteristic of Islamic devotion to Allah. The Witnesses put it in this manner:

Strangest of all ideas is the idea that it is in the hands of men to accelerate or retard the accomplishment of God's great and glorious designs. To hurry God's movements; what comment is adequate to such towering pride.[35]

This attitude naturally prohibits participation in initiating social change. To such an extreme did Rutherford carry his idea of Destiny that he cautioned his followers against taking any part in a social struggle of

---

[32] *Watch Tower*, June, 1883.

[33] According to one Witness, "Often I have arrived late at night, the train being unduly delayed, at a lone station, but true to his promise, the Lord never leaves me in the lurch. On every occasion he put it into the heart of someone to help me." *Ibid.*, Jan., 1924.

[34] *Ibid.*, Jan., 1882.　　　　　　　　　　[35] *Ibid.*, Sept., 1896.

which God had already foreordained the winners and the losers. In 1938, speaking directly about the rise of the totalitarian governments in Europe and Asia, Mr. Rutherford said: "The Totalitarian combine is going to get control of England and America. You cannot prevent it. Do not try. Your safety is on the Lord's side." [36]

This on-rolling Destiny has bewildered many present-day Witnesses who now doubt whether such a prediction can ever be realized. For the most part, they do not worry about the course of the present world struggle, because their hopes are pinned upon final purposes only remotely connected with it. They exemplify the description of the poet Stoddard:

> We have two lives about us,
> Two worlds in which we dwell,
> Within us, and without us,
> Alternate Heaven and Hell;
> Without the somber Real,
> Within our heart of hearts the beautiful Ideal.[37]

When all of the nations of the earth lie in devastation as a result of the widespread slaughter and the "scorched earth policy," the appointed time of the Witnesses will have arrived. It is then that they will come into their "land flowing with milk and honey." In this ideal state no evil will enter: breweries will be closed; prostitution will be stopped; war instruments will be destroyed; banks and brokerage houses will be closed; landlords will be no more; there will be no disease, no taxes, no worry, no poor people, no death, nor any other Stygian evil which the true believer cares to add to the list.[38]

Although "the New Jerusalem" is to be established upon the earth, none of the areas of the earth's surface will remain as they now are. One evening, as I was walking home from a meeting with the leader of a Company in New York City, he looked up at the gaunt buildings on every side and said: "See those buildings? They won't be here when the theocracy comes. Smell that air? God will purify it when the theocracy comes." He went on to tell me of the conception which he had of that future. He thought that all of New York City and other large cities like it would have to be destroyed; in their places Jehovah would raise beautiful green grass. No one would need to work, so that all would have

---

[36] Rutherford, *Face the Facts*, p. 27.
[37] Richard H. Stoddard, *Poems* (New York, 1880), p. 3: "The Castle in the Air."
[38] Rutherford, *The Kingdom*, pp. 18–19.

plenty of opportunity to walk upon the green grass and to rest and sleep in the open fields. The temperature would always be warm enough to be pleasant to all, but never would one perspire. I commented on the lack of trees in the wide-open fields that he described, but he replied that space was more valuable to him than trees. There seemed to be no provision in his scheme for homes and little concern for family life. Everyone would take care of himself and a high degree of solitude would be enjoyed by all. My Witness friend did not know whether people would have to eat, but he was sure they would have to sleep.

In this Utopia, everything would be taken care of by the ruling princes come back from the grave. David would be especially popular among the youngsters, but all of the Old Testament heroes would be loved and respected. The people would not see Jesus, however, as he would be "too busy" to go about in his new creation, but he would certainly know all about the affairs of the perfect society. Furthermore, there would be no reason to meet Jesus personally, for the ruling princes would tell such tales about him that the people would be satisfied merely with the hearing. Things would run along in this fashion day in and day out; no one would care about time, for "a thousand years will seem as a day." How do the Witnesess know these things? They say with Dante: "Like one who has imperfect vision, we see the things which are remote from us."

Whether this particular version of the future of society intrigues the minds of all of the Witnesses may be seriously doubted. Probably there are as many versions of the divinely created order of things to come as there are Witnesses. Each reads into his interpretation of the destined future the things he most desires and lacks. Some are impressed with the natural surroundings of their heavenly dream-state; others are interested in marriage and the raising of children; others are chiefly concerned with leisure-time activities. All unite, however, in believing that the kingdom of Jehovah is close at hand. All are agreed that only Destiny can accomplish the goal.

This dream activity of the Witnesses is believed as any idealized hope is, and provides them with vast driving power in their service work. Probably the dream has been one of the influential factors in converting to the movement large numbers of people who have experienced little else than emotional repression and material want. By a similar hope the Mormons of earlier years were driven across a broad continent to realize their dream in a salt-lake valley. The Witnesses of our day have derived energy by channelizing their imagery along organizational lines. They have striven to establish a world-wide, closely knit, "perfect," authoritarian organization in which every Witness is linked with his fellow believers in a divinely implemented program. Obviously, they desire to convert all to their faith, that all may enjoy the dream. They do not mind hardships, because they are convinced that at the end of their rainbow exists a sizable pot of gold.

O, that prize is so glorious, so wonderful, and the kingdom is so near; what manner of people ought we to be in all holy conduct! Praise the Lord, we are almost home! The lights of the Eternal City are almost discernible, and soon we shall be home and at rest.[39]

The theology of the Jehovah's Witnesses has a definite bearing on the lives of the Witnesses, as has been suggested. One gets the impression, however, after living with the Witnesses for a period, that they could just as well manage all that they are doing for and receiving from the movement if some other absolutist theology were to be substituted.

While the doctrine of Destiny is an important Witness belief, there are many others which give character and meaning to the organization's program. An official statement of belief appears regularly on the first page of *The Watch Tower* for the convenience of Witnesses who wish to refresh themselves as to the correct formula for obtaining salvation. Although the form of the statement has changed several times in the history of the movement, its meaning has remained about the same. In practice the theology is colored by personal interpretations and emphases. What is important to one Witness may be less important to another. But what each appeals to as the official statement of his beliefs reads as follows:

THE SCRIPTURES CLEARLY TEACH

THAT JEHOVAH is the only true God and is from everlasting to everlasting, the Maker of heaven and earth and the Giver of life to his creatures; that the Logos was the beginning of his creation, and his active agent in the creation of all other things, and is now the Lord Jesus Christ in glory, clothed with all power in heaven and earth, as the Chief Executive Officer of Jehovah;

[39] *Watch Tower*, Dec., 1913.

THAT GOD created the earth for man, created perfect man for the earth and placed him upon it; that man willfully disobeyed God's law and was sentenced to death; that by reason of Adam's wrong act all men are born sinners and without the right to life;

THAT THE LOGOS was made human as the man Jesus and suffered death in order to produce the ransom or redemptive price for obedient ones of mankind; that God raised up Jesus divine and exalted him to heaven above every other creature and above every name and clothed him with all power and authority;

THAT JEHOVAH'S ORGANIZATION is a Theocracy called Zion, and that Christ Jesus is the Chief Officer thereof and is the rightful King of the world; that the anointed and faithful followers of Christ Jesus are children of Zion, members of Jehovah's organization, and are his witnesses whose duty and privilege it is to testify to the supremacy of Jehovah, declare his purposes toward mankind as expressed in the Bible, and to bear the fruits of the Kingdom before all who will hear;

THAT THE OLD WORLD ended in A. D. 1914, and the Lord Jesus Christ has been placed by Jehovah upon his throne of authority, has ousted Satan from heaven and is proceeding to the establishment of the "new earth" of the New World;

THAT THE RELIEF and blessings of the peoples of earth can come only by and through Jehovah's kingdom under Christ, which has now begun; that the Lord's next great act is the destruction of Satan's organization and the complete establishment of righteousness in the earth, and that under the Kingdom the people of good-will that survive Armageddon shall carry out the divine mandate to "fill the earth" with a righteous race.

A member of the Board of Directors of the Society told me that thus far all attempts by outsiders to discover the real significance of the Society's theology had failed because the persons making them had not perceived "the inner and secret meanings" which are open only to true believers. Therefore, one cannot validate "the truth" until one has accepted it. Obviously, when one accepts it, there is no further question of its validity. The Board member gave me a mimeographed copy of a decision handed down in 1938 in an Appellate Court of South Africa, in the case of Bulawayo *vs.* Oliver Maidstone Kabungo. In preparing his decision, the judge supposedly made an intensive study of Mr. Rutherford's books and tried to outline the essential beliefs of the Jehovah's Witnesses. This summary was cited by the Board member as "the finest I have seen":

God, Jehovah, is the supreme ruler. Satan, then known as Lucifer, was originally part of God's organization and the perfect man was placed under him. Lucifer rebelled against God, who then changed his name and thereafter gave him the names Satan, Serpent, Dragon and Devil. Satan set up his own organization in challenge to God and through that organization he has for centuries ruled the world. In thus ruling and controlling the world Satan uses three elements, namely, commercial, political and religious. Of these the author singles out the last for his fiercest attacks. Organized Christianity or Christendom, as the religion of nations, is under the control of Satan, whose great instrument it is for deceiving the people, for seducing and misleading them and keeping them superstitiously in subjection. All nations and all their rulers and governments are included in Satan's organization, the British Empire being specially mentioned in several of the works, as being amongst the worse.

To a world so burdened and oppressed relief will come. Jesus, the head of God's organization will again come to earth and will destroy entirely Satan's organization. The destruction, which is frequently characterized as slaughter by the sword, will be effected solely by Christ and his angels and it is nowhere suggested that earthly beings will take any active part in it.

There are, however, millions of people of good will in Christendom, who are honest of heart and who have a desire to see righteousness in the earth. These are to be informed of God's purpose, that they may take their stand on His side and thereby escape the great slaughter which will shortly follow. The information is to be given by persons styled "Jehovah's witnesses," by means, principally, of the distribution of publications such as those now being considered. When this preaching or testifying to the world is completed, and immediately following it, the "slaughter work" will begin.

The second coming of Christ has already commenced. In 1914 God set him on his Heavenly throne, thus enabling him to drive Satan from Heaven. In 1918 Christ entered God's temple and offered himself as King and rightful Ruler of the earth.

And so the great day is at hand, when will take place the great slaughter resulting in the final elimination of Satan and all his works. After that, under the Government of God, there will be an end of misrule and oppression and there will be peace in the world. Such is the theme, with variations, and purporting to rest on Biblical statements and prophecies, which run throughout all the publications.

It is stated that all present governments are hopeless and can hold out no hope for suffering humanity; that it is no use looking to them as they are doomed to destruction. In every publication, however, people are advised and urged not to join any earthly organization and not to take part in any fighting or violence. They are told that if they dissociate themselves from earthly governments and accept the Word of God and preach it, they will be saved. Such, in short, is the nature of the publications with which I have to deal in this application.

Neither the *Watch Tower* statement nor the foregoing summary contains any mention of the ceremonial observances of the movement. In proselytizing, the Witnesses claim that they have no religious rites and generally insist that such observances are part of "religion." Ceremonies are considered by many as "superstitiousness." Possibly the belief that all religious observances are "superstitious" arose from the Society's desire to eliminate the large number of ceremonies which characterize some religions. The Witnesses feel that the worship of Jehovah excludes any reliance upon ceremonies. They are of the opinion that the first commandment of the Decalogue forbids them from engaging in any practice which tends to distract the participant from his solitary obligation to the Deity. The celebration of a day such as "Mother's Day" is regarded by the Witnesses as distracting from their primary responsibility to Jehovah. "Mother's Day," according to Rutherford, is "just another one of Satan's means." [40]

The Witnesses also believe that Christmas should not be celebrated because it is an admixture of a Christian idea and a pagan setting. The older Witnesses still observe Christmas because Mr. Russell nowhere spoke against it, but the younger ones believe that the pagan origins of the day make it unworthy of their attention. The objections are centered largely against the lavish giving of gifts as a practice which does not represent "original" Christianity. Moreover, the proverbial Christmas tree is called an "antitype" of the tree which grew in Nimrod's "backyard" upon his death and symbolizes the inherent vitality of evil. [41] Having a Christmas tree in one's home signifies that one is willing to worship the evil descending all the way from Nimrod. The lights on the tree are said to have been derived from a pagan custom of one of the Germanic tribes called "Belts" (probably "Celts" is meant). Centuries ago this pagan tribe, recognizing the power of Satan, used to decorate evergreen trees with candles to give light in the village square during the winter months. The light from the candles was intended to chase away the evil spirits of the night. The use of lights on Christmas trees by anyone today signifies his intention to live as a pagan, with the hope that the tree lights

[40] *Ibid.*, May, 1940.   [41] Genesis 10: 8, 9; I Chronicles 1: 10; Micah 5: 6.

will dispel the evil spirits. All this is too much for the Witnesses. It smacks so much of Satan that they will have none of it.

In 1940, one day shortly before Christmas, I was seated at the breakfast table with a Witness couple, when the wife asked me whether I was intending to celebrate Christmas. Without waiting for my answer, she continued by telling me about the terrible struggle she had to abandon the custom. She said that her husband was not so greatly affected as she was when they ceased celebrating the day. The couple had come from northern Europe soon after their marriage, and carried with them many recollections of Christmas with their families in the old country. The wife declared that she would never again celebrate Christmas, but added with a shrug of her shoulders, "I should worry. The kingdom may be here before Christmas."

Nevertheless, certain ceremonies are recognized and observed by the Witnesses at regular intervals. The "high" ceremonies of the movement at its founding were three: Baptism, the Memorial Supper, and Sunday.[42] In recent years the ceremonial and sacred character of Sunday has been lost by most Witnesses who regard it merely as another day in which they can engage in service work. The practices of baptism and of the Memorial Supper, however, are still faithfully observed.

In the early days of the movement there was some discussion over the number of ceremonies which the Bible permitted. Some of the early converts felt that they should practice the ceremony of feet washing because to them the obligation was laid upon every Christian by Jesus' example and words. Pastor Russell, however, ruled out feet washing, saying that true believers could accept it only in a symbolic way.[43] Others felt that the funeral service should be an important occasion, but this was also dismissed by Mr. Russell as giving too much emphasis to a fact which in itself is not pleasant. As a result, the Witness funeral service is generally unpretentious. Similar to those conducted by many non-liturgical churches,[44] it usually consists of several passages of Scripture, possibly a talk, and prayer. The leader may be a local Witness who has been selected or has volunteered for the occasion. The procedure, however, is declared by the Witnesses to be nonceremonial.

Of the two primary ceremonies (baptism and the Memorial Supper) now observed by the Witnesses, that of baptism has changed with time. In the first few years of the group's history the practice of baptism was

[42] *Watch Tower*, March, 1896. [43] *Ibid.*, March, 1898. [44] *Ibid.*, Nov., 1879.

quite simple; later it grew more formal, but in recent years has become less so. In the early days when the number of adherents was small, Mr. Russell advised all who were interested to write him personally. Accordingly, in 1880 he was approached by various followers concerning the problem of baptism. Usually he arranged for a baptismal service to be held in conjunction with his lectures in various towns and cities. If candidates did not care to await his arrival, he suggested that they "baptize one another, or get a minister from the Christian Disciple Church." [45]

In later years, the two ceremonies of the movement were brought together by the fact that baptism was generally administered just before the Memorial Supper.[46] Some members objected to the double observance, however, saying it made the meeting inordinately long. As a result they were thereafter observed separately; but because in recent years the Memorial Supper has been approached by too many unbaptized converts, baptism before the Supper has been renewed.

The practice of baptism was introduced in a special ceremony at the first national convention, held in Chicago in 1893. The candidates convened in a Baptist church, dressed in white robes, and were immersed by Mr. Russell.

At the height of Mr. Russell's popularity, baptism was usually administered in local Protestant churches. In these cases the local minister, most often a Disciple, would immerse the believer. Baptists were seldom asked to officiate because the Witnesses felt that they would not do so unless the person immersed subsequently became a member of the Baptist church. Those who were baptized wore flowing gowns of white to signify the purity of the convert's heart. Later, the wearing of special garb was discontinued, as an undesirable ostentation. During Mr. Russell's lifetime, baptism was also administered at the international conventions. At such times candidates met at a church suited for the purpose and were immersed by Mr. Russell, while hundreds of believers looked on. Today the service has become less formal. Baptisms are held chiefly at the international conventions, but never in churches. In 1940, at Detroit, approximately 3,500 were immersed in the public pool at Eastwood Park. The ceremony was performed by Witness friends of those baptized. All were dressed in bathing suits, so that a good swim could follow the cleansing ceremony. Baptisms are sometimes held at "assem-

[45] *Ibid.*, Nov., 1880.   [46] *Ibid.*, May, 1897.

blies," if proper facilities are available. A zone assembly in New York City used an indoor, public swimming pool for the purpose. On the whole, the Witnesses are inclined to wait for a special convocation before requesting baptism; the ceremony is seldom performed in the local Company.

The Witnesses believe that only adult, converted, true believers may be baptized. Babies cannot believe "the truth," therefore, it is not right to baptize them. Russell gave specific injunction to those who had been baptized before conversion that they must be rebaptized; [47] the earlier ceremony was sinful because it was performed in ignorance of "the truth."

Any symbolism, such as the power of baptism to wash away the past sins of the believer, is considered as "superstitious." Witnesses are baptized simply "because Jesus said that every Christian should be." They do not look upon the experience as contributing anything to their spiritual development; it is simply a necessary rite, full of fun, and guaranteeing one's status as a real Witness. No problem arises over the necessity of baptizing people too old or too infirm to be immersed. Witnesses have informed me that in such cases the person is assured that the ceremony "really doesn't matter," but if he insists, they are willing to "sprinkle" (or, as it has been called, "christen") him.

The Memorial Supper as practiced by Witnesses corresponds more closely to what Protestants term "Communion" or "the Lord's Supper," than to what Roman Catholics call "the Holy Eucharist." The Memorial Supper "was given to us to take the place of the Jewish Paschal Supper and to be celebrated at the corresponding time each year." [48] At first, it was observed only at the central headquarters in Allegheny, Pennsylvania. Later, as more converts were won, small groups throughout the country met to celebrate it in their own towns and cities. In the beginning Mr. Russell thought that in as much as Jesus used only one loaf of bread for his memorial supper, his faithful followers should do likewise. As the group increased in numbers, however, this early doctrine was changed so that more than one loaf and, in some cases, "water-crackers" could be used. At first the true believers were encouraged to sip unfermented grape juice or fermented raisin juice. The use of raisin juice, however, caused many objections, since Witnesses who had been violent drinkers before conversion and had been "saved" from the practice by their conversion, might with one sip be led back to drink and to a subsequent

[47] *Ibid.*, Sept., 1882.   [48] *Ibid.*, March, 1894.

life of sin. The objections caused Mr. Russell to reconsider the propriety
of alcohol in the Memorial Supper. He did not conclude that it was forbidden; careful Bible study led him to believe that wine was more "biblical" than grape or raisin juice. In *The Watch Tower* he wrote:

We have regretted since our last issue that we recommended raisin juice as
a substitute for wine. Upon further reflection it seems to us that WINE is the
only proper element or emblem. All Scriptural references to wine indicate that
it was of a sort that would intoxicate.[49]

This statement of the use of wine merely brought further reverberations
from his followers, until (after continued study) Mr. Russell advised
in desperation that wine was perhaps not "the proper emblem" and suggested that unfermented grape juice be used once more. Lately the Witnesses have again returned to the use of wine.

The Memorial Supper is conducted today according to the familiar
Protestant pattern. Prayers and Scripture readings accompany the service, but no singing. The "elders," usually Pioneers, are those Witnesses
who are recognized by the Company as being especially devout. The
"body" and "blood" are passed to the participants by the elders. In former
times, the Witnesses seriously discussed whether the elders should partake of the bread and wine before distributing them. Some felt that this
was the proper procedure because the elders would then have been purified
before distributing "the elements." To others, less ritual-minded, the
Supper denoted only the carrying out of Jehovah's will; to them "it
looked funny" to see the elders partaking of the Supper before the other
communicants. The problem has never been solved to the satisfaction of
all the Witnesses.

In the former days the group celebrating the Memorial Supper read
from *The Watch Tower,* as is evidenced in an early report: "After prayer
and singing together we read articles from 'The Watch Tower.' We all
joined in reading the Scripture proofs, and then partook of the bread
and wine according to the word." [50] In those days the Memorial Supper was celebrated as near as possible (in the opinion of the Witnesses)
to the exact day and hour in which it was instituted by Jesus.[51] Today,
however, this aspect is disregarded because of the number of people
involved and the inconvenience caused.

The local Companies formerly reported the number of participants

---

[49] *Ibid.,* May, 1882.   [50] *Ibid.,* May, 1885.   [51] *Ibid.,* April, 1885.

in the Memorial Supper to the central office, and the total figures were published in *The Watch Tower*. For example, the number of participants in 1924, a period of comparative decline, was 61,911.[52] Never has the group reported more than 75,000 participants, although in recent years it has refused to make the figures public, probably because to a certain extent the number of participants in the Memorial Supper corresponds to the number of very active Witnesses.

Through the Memorial Supper some of the Witnesses become especially devoted to "the cause." The Supper unifies the group's emotions and purposes. While the rite of baptism is taken rather lightly, the Memorial Supper is always celebrated in a deeply thoughtful manner. Some members feel particularly close to Jesus during and after the observance of "the feast." In the words of one Witness:

I used to like Christ, felt very grateful to him for forgiving my sins and for the peace I even then felt, and was willing to do a great many things for him. Now I think I can truly say I love him with all my being; and what a wonderful change has come over my whole life! Truly he is the one altogether lovely.[53]

Others have the feeling that they are on much more intimate terms with God, or, as one woman called him, "our very dear Jehovah." [54] The use of the phrase indicates the extent to which the original meaning of the theological concepts has been modified and also the degree to which the experience of the Memorial Supper has affected the believer.

[52] *Ibid.*, July, 1924.   [53] *Ibid.*, April, 1896.   [54] *Ibid.*, April, 1929.

Attitudes and Relations

To THE OBSERVER, the Jehovah's Witnesses seem to have made "hate a
religion." [1] Whatever else the Witnesses may believe, they do somehow
feel that the whole world is arrayed against them, and respond with
resentment, hatred, and bitterness. They believe they owe the world
nothing, and from the world they want nothing, for it is evil and not in
any sense a positive part of the divine purpose. The list of the resentments is long; actually it includes all of "Satan's organization" which in
turn may be defined as any institution or person opposed to "the Lord's
organization." By "the Lord's organization" the Witnesses generally
mean the Watch Tower Bible and Tract Society of which Charles T.
Russell was the founder and Joseph Franklin Rutherford the late head.
Any individual or institution not in harmony with "the Lord's organization" is inspired of Satan and is to be hated to the utmost by all true
believers. [2]

Those who have met with actual opposition in the pursuance of their
duties have readily made known their experiences to other Witnesses,
who in turn have spread the information to many others. In this way
stories circulate among them of various persecutions in all parts of this
country and indeed throughout the world. If these stories are of sufficient interest to the entire flock they are published on the back cover
of *The Watch Tower*. The greatly increased number of "field experiences" of this kind carried by *The Watch Tower* in recent years signifies
the degree to which the Witnesses have been subjected to violent opposition.

Attacks on the Society are considered by Witnesses as attacks upon
themselves. A Witness from Tennessee declares: "The things that are
written and said against the Society I take as personally said about me,
because I fully endorse all that is being said and done by the Society." [3]
Since the Witnesses view opposition in such a personal way and since they
seek to defend the Society against all attacks, they often find themselves
persecuted by those who oppose the movement in the countries where it
functions. In Germany alone, in 1937, Mr. Rutherford claimed that approximately two thousand Witnesses were interned in concentration
camps for their opposition to Hitler, [4] and a few years later raised this

[1] Stanley High, "Armageddon, Inc.," *Saturday Evening Post*, Sept. 14, 1940.
[2] Guy A. Aldred, *Armageddon, Incorporated*, p. 26.   [3] *Watch Tower*, March, 1926.
[4] Rutherford, *Armageddon*, p. 28.

estimate to about six thousand. In most of the other European countries faithful Witnesses have been imprisoned. Often their fate has been worse: at times Witnesses have been slain for refusing to salute a national flag, for refusing to fight, or for refusing to use terms of address considered proper by a special elite group within the nation; and reports of sterilization of some Witnesses in Germany reached the United States before this country formally entered the war.

Moreover, persecution of the Witnesses has not been confined to Europe. In this country the records of the Society and of the American Civil Liberties Union show that in 1940 these two groups reported to the Department of Justice over 335 cases in which Witnesses were subjected to mob violence. In a sworn affidavit from Arizona, one Witness describes his experience while he was trying to distribute the Society's literature:

On Wednesday evening, June 19th, 1940, my dad and I drove to Ash Fork from Williams to contact two fellow workers at a friend's house. I drove up in front of the house and went up on the porch when three men stepped into the yard and up on the porch and said, "Are you looking for anyone?"—and then, "Will you salute the flag?" and when I replied that I respected the flag but was consecrated to do God's will and did not salute or attribute salvation to the flag they cried, "Nazi spy!" knocked me down, beat me badly, and finally knocked me out—then dragged and pushed me across the street to a service station and again tried to make me salute the flag. I was dizzy, befuddled and don't clearly remember anything except that a considerable crowd had gathered yelling "Nazi spy!—Heil Hitler!— String him up!—Chop off his head."

A deputy sheriff appeared later. He took me to a local jail and put my dad and I in a cell, as he said, "to protect you from the mob and to rest you up." [5]

In 1940 such cases reached what the American Civil Liberties Union considers the peak. The Union has gone voluntarily to the aid of Witnesses in need of legal help and has prepared a booklet, *The Persecution of Jehovah's Witnesses*, which to date, although devoid of any lengthy sociological and psychological analysis, is the best source (aside from the Witnesses themselves) for studying the persecutions of Witnesses in the United States. This booklet shows that the newspapers in some cities and

[5] American Civil Liberties Union, *The Persecution of the Jehovah's Witnesses*, p. 6.

towns have violently opposed distribution of Witness literature. Residents of these communities undoubtedly feel that a kind of sanction for mob violence is given them by such opposition. In some localities the police have failed to intervene. At Litchfield, Illinois, for example, the law officers refused to quell an unruly crowd attacking a group of Witnesses until the mobsters began to beat the women.

Eight months after the publication of the Union's booklet, the legal staff of the Society prepared a pamphlet entitled *Jehovah's Servants Defended*. Although this pamphlet also seeks the prevention of further persecution, its content is almost completely different. It tries to show, among other things, that the laws of the land support the Witnesses in the door-to-door distribution of their literature, and is construed by the Society as being a manual on the rights of its members in service work.

The American Civil Liberties Union has offered rewards of $500 for the arrest and conviction of any persons persecuting the Witnesses, and on the whole the results of this offer have been beneficial. In cases where local authorities have been unable or unwilling to handle the situation, the Union and the legal staff of the Society have appealed to the Department of Justice. The Federal Bureau of Investigation has examined about one hundred cases in which the local authorities failed to prevent or stop persecutions, or even took part in them.

The words of Solicitor General Francis Biddle, spoken in a nationwide broadcast in 1940, are familiar to many as expressing the attitude of the government toward the persecution of the Witnesses:

A religious sect known as Jehovah's Witnesses have been repeatedly set upon and beaten. They had committed no crime; but the mob adjudged they had, and meted out mob punishment. The Attorney General has ordered an immediate investigation of these outrages.

The people must be alert and watchful, and above all cool and sane. Since mob violence will make the government's task infinitely more difficult, it will not be tolerated. We shall not defeat the Nazi evil by emulating its methods.

To counteract persecution, the Witnesses throughout their history have devised theoretical distinctions between themselves and their foes. These make the enmity more understandable and bearable to the ordinary Witness. Mr. Rutherford used a common religious technique of classifying people and applied it relentlessly. He said: "The two classes are clearly and distinctly marked out by the Scriptures, one doomed to absolute and complete destruction, the other having a possibility of recovery." [6] These two groups are the familiar "saved" and "unsaved." All Witnesses are "in the true light"; while those who do not believe will be completely destroyed. This formula was seized upon eagerly by the Witnesses and for years has been one of their dominant ideas. It provides them with an overly simple technique for examining—and judging—the ideas and relations of others.

The stress upon impassable differences between believer and non-believer has welded the organization together into a single fighting unit. Witnesses differing in financial and social status, in color, and even in creed, unite in the face of a common foe and seek by all means both to protect those of their own special group and to advocate the complete destruction of the common enemy. Thus many Witnesses work with monumental courage against the forces seeking their defeat.

The theme of common enemies reached its peak of acceptance in 1937 with the publication of *Enemies* by Mr. Rutherford. The definitions herein employed to describe the enemies of the movement are all very ancient and very traditional. From this book and from other sources the characteristic traits of the enemy can be summarized.

First, he is conceived of as being "far below the standard of perfect human nature." [7] That is to say that the enemy is unacquainted with "civilized" ways of living and fighting; in the present intersocietal war he is "the barbarian"; his mode of life is "unbearable for decent human beings." [8]

Second, because of his intrinsically subhuman condition, he is labeled "strange." [9] Since his way of life is diametrically opposed to that of the Witnesses, he is necessarily "queer."

Third, the enemies do not understand or practice any morality.[10] Rutherford's *Enemies* characterizes them as "racketeers," as "artful, wily, and cunning." They use any scheme "to gain an unfair advantage over others." The Witness view is not that their enemies possess a different morality but that they possess no morality at all.

Fourth, the enemies use secret methods of attack; they are sometimes invisible.[11] Witnesses are warned that the battle may be with intangible factors that, if unconsidered, may cause defeat.

---

[6] Rutherford, *Angels*, p. 56.
[8] *Ibid.*, April, 1933.
[10] *Ibid.*, June, 1896.
[7] *Watch Tower*, April, 1897.
[9] *Ibid.*, May, 1938.
[11] Rutherford, *Enemies*, pp. 305–306.

The relations between believers and nonbelievers necessarily call for militant tactics. A little group of Witnesses wrote to Mr. Rutherford: "We wish to go on record as to our determination to fight shoulder to shoulder with you in this great battle." [12] Another Witness writes that he is thankful for Rutherford's "love of the little army in the field." [13] If one understands the Witness conception of their enemies, one can appreciate the solid affinity between the partial military structure of the organization and the attempt to lead a religious life.

Mr. Russell sometimes grouped together different organizations whom the true believer must hate. In one passage he lists theosophy, Christian Science, and spiritism as being in the "popular current toward infidelity." [14] In another place he says: "Freemasonry, Odd Fellowship, Trade Unions, Guilds, and Trusts, all are evil, hiding the sinful from the full light of God's grace." [15] Although Mr. Russell did group opposing factions together occasionally, nevertheless he never spoke of them as being deliberately united. More often, he particularized the individuals and organizations which opposed him. A member of the Roman Catholic Church was described as "a lawless Roman Catholic rumseller." [16] "Bible critics" were criticized because they taught the people "evolution," which to the Witnesses was one of the cardinal tools of Satan.[17] Missionaries were opposed because they were "dupes" of the churches in the extension of the churches' power.[18] Physicians were accused of taking unfair advantage of their patients, and Witnesses often refused to call them even to have their children vaccinated.[19]

Later the paramount idea was that the small, individual evils retarding the Witnesses in their service work were merely the result of one evil person—Satan. In the period immediately following Mr. Rutherford's accession to leadership, all evils were attributed to "his Satanic majesty." Thus the battle of the Witnesses was not of a mundane but of a celestial character, of cosmic proportions. Even until quite late in his life, Mr. Rutherford was forced to remind the Witnesses of this view of the origin of their enemies: "In recent years 'The Watch Tower' has time and again declared that we have no fight with men. Our fight is with Satan, and a host of wicked angels operating with him." [20]

[12] *Watch Tower*, Sept., 1929.   [13] *Ibid.*, Oct., 1929.
[14] Russell, *Studies in the Scriptures*, IV, 66.   [15] *Ibid.*, II, 139.
[16] *Watch Tower*, Jan., 1889.   [17] Russell, *Studies in the Scriptures*, III, 167.
[18] *Ibid.*, III, 177.   [19] *Consolation*, Feb., 1929.   [20] Rutherford, *Angels*, p. 50.

In 1926 Mr. Rutherford published a book, *Deliverance*, which attempts to give, in effect, a short outline of general history. Mr. Rutherford here reveals how every good intention of Jehovah has been "overreached" by Satan. He speaks of the manner in which men in times past conceived evil, but he also discloses the true source of evil as he sees it:

Now it is due time for the people to see and to understand the truth; and particularly to see that all the warfare amongst themselves, the conflicts among religious systems, and the crimes and wickedness that stalk about in the earth, all these unrighteous things originated with Satan who has used these agencies to turn the minds of the people away from God.[21]

According to Rutherford, Jehovah has given over the running of the earth and its affairs to Satan, but soon the Deity will come in majesty and glory to force the final victory. Thus, even man's highest aspirations, including those expressed in historical religions, are the result of a demonic force outside both himself and nature, a force which really controls the world in this age.

In the period in which the evils of the world were ascribed to Satan primarily and only secondarily to his instruments, the evil institutions of this world, the Witnesses were inclined to show a type of apathy toward their persecutors which later was called to their shame. Witnesses today still can recall the time when they were instructed not to resist evil. Gradually, however, the primacy of Satan was minimized and specific organizations were deemed the greatest and strongest foes of all true believers. The stage for this newer emphasis was set in Rutherford's *Enemies*, the very title of which signifies the plurality of foes. It was in 1937 that the Witnesses first coined the phrase which they have stressed ever since—"Religion is a racket." By this was and still is meant that religion is evil not because of a demonic controlling force which uses it to pervert the bulk of mankind, but that in itself religion is evil.[22] In proof of this assertion few references are made to the Bible, naturally, but emphasis is laid upon certain beliefs—as the immorality and selfishness of the clergy—popular among Witnesses. In regard to the Roman Catholic Church, a sharp differentiation was made between the priesthood and the laity: the former being intensely wicked, the latter, capable

[21] Rutherford, *Deliverance*, p. 150.
[22] "The greatest racket ever invented and practiced is that of religion." Rutherford, *Enemies*, p. 144.

of much good.[23] Also, in this period, the discrimination between "religion" and "Christianity" became current. In regard to government, the political leaders of the nations were no longer held to be mere instruments of an evil spiritual force, personified as Satan, but were conceived as being wicked by their own choice and responsibility. In a sense, this latest development is in accord with a trend which has been apparent in religious forms for some time, namely, the gradual substitution of "natural" for "supernatural" causes, and the reorientation of religious meanings into a more scientific framework.

Witnesses no longer believe that they must not resist evil, but feel compelled, as occasion demands, to take active part in forcibly defending themselves and their "rights." What happened, for example, on the 25th of June, 1939, in Madison Square Garden would not have been possible in 1925. Mr. Rutherford described the event as follows:

Persons who oppose God's kingdom had repeatedly made threats that they would break up that assembly, and these threats have been brought to the attention of the Lord's people. Even the police officers had been notified of such threats. On the day of the meeting several hundred people, of the wicked ones, entered Madison Square Garden after the program had begun, and a violent attempt to "break-up" that meeting ensued. Ushers, whose assigned duty was to keep order, commanded the disturbers to stop their disturbance or else leave the room. Instead of complying with that request the disturbers violently assaulted the ushers. Some of the ushers in their God-given and lawful rights resisted such assaults and used reasonable and necessary force to repel such wrongful assaults. In doing so the ushers acted strictly within their rights and in the performance of their duty and certainly have the approval of the Lord in so doing. The ushers were not using carnal weapons in order to preach the gospel, but they were using force to compel the enemy to desist in efforts to prevent the preaching of the gospel.[24]

Witness wrath turns upon the American Legion as a minority group of superpatriots who "attempt to make and enforce their own laws, which deny the rights of the people." [25] The attitude of individual Witnesses against the American Legion is more bitter than that officially expressed in the literature. The various flag-saluting laws, as well as those compelling military service, are laid by the Witnesses to the door of this organization.

[23] *Ibid.*, p. 205.   [24] Rutherford, *Religion*, p. 295.
[25] Rutherford, *Armageddon*, p. 38.

The Jews also are hated by the Witnesses. Although this feeling is common among them, it appears strange at first glance, inasmuch as the movement appeals to many Jews. But all who have joined "the Lord's organization" are precious in the sight of Jehovah and are fellow members of a special human group; thus, converted Jews are made welcome, often with the idea that they are "the chosen people." The official literature terms the Jews outside the movement "blind" because they do not accept "the truth." [26]

Prevalent among the Witnesses is the notion that all Jews are rich. Even refugees who have escaped to this country from persecution abroad are believed to have brought "scads of money" with them. One Witness told me fantastic tales about the apparent luxury within some of the homes of Jewish refugees that he had visited. The affluence of the refugees, according to this Witness, is hidden from most people because they do not have the opportunity which he and his fellow workers have of visiting all kinds of homes.

In spite of this generally unfavorable attitude, which is, indeed, sometimes shared by Jewish Witnesses themselves, the movement is able to satisfy its Jewish members, who find in its theology the natural, developed expression of essential Judaism.

The official literature of the movement does not say much about Negroes. In regard to salvation, Mr. Rutherford stated: "The blackest man from Africa will have the same opportunity as the white man of America. There will be no race distinction." [27] This attitude appears constantly in the official pronouncements of local Companies: all people are eligible to any office within the organization; anyone can become a Publisher or a Pioneer. But seldom do the Witnesses feel as did a white Pioneer in the South: "I wish to say that when the kingdom is fully established the colored people will be in the majority of those who march in the kingdom." [28] More often the Negroes are accepted and tolerated, but not taken into intimate confidence, and there are no Negroes in influential positions in the organizational set-up. They are not encouraged to enter into the service work as Pioneers except in areas which are predominantly Negroid. Once in the history of the movement the Society's leader specifically asked colored Witnesses not to apply for positions as Pioneers:

[26] Rutherford, *Jews*, pp. 8–9. [27] *Ibid.*, p. 7. [28] *Watch Tower*, Nov., 1935.

The reason is that so far as we are able to judge, colored people have less education than whites—many of them quite insufficient to permit them to profit by reading our literature. Our conclusion, therefore, is based upon the supposition that reading matter distributed to a colored congregation would be more than half wasted, and a very small percentage indeed likely to yield good results.[29]

The shortcomings of "a religion of the book," however, have never been officially recognized by the Society, even when it admits the inability of vast numbers of people to comprehend what it is teaching.

Witness resentment focuses also upon a triad which is usually termed "the religious, commercial, and political combine"—three elements in society that are united in opposing "the Lord's organization." The "combine" is not new in the literature of the movement, for it appeared even in Russell's time.[30] By joining the religious, commercial, and political interests together, the Witnesses are able to express a total resentment more powerful and coherent than that elicited by the three singly.

The mistrust of all religions is one of the prime factors in the efforts of Witnesses to convert others. It also explains in part their relations with an important area of society, namely, religious institutions. In a time when religious organizations are feeling the threat of a common foe, whatever it may be called—paganism, naturalism, force, irreligion—the Jehovah's Witnesses have consistently refused to join with those who would be their friends. The Society is not represented, for example, upon the Board of Directors of the American Bible Society, an organization which exists solely for the publication and distribution of the Bible. It will have no part in the Federal Council of the Churches of Christ in America, and believes that group to be one of the "tools of Satan." [31] On the same ground, the Jehovah's Witnesses refuse to support local churches or such groups as the Y.M.C.A. or the Y.M.H.A.

An especial animosity is directed toward the Roman Catholic Church as a world-wide organization, although the Witnesses are in no sense tolerant of Protestants. Indeed, Mr. Rutherford believed that the Protestant nations are more responsible for present conditions than are the Roman Catholic.[32] Even the Fundamentalists or conservative Protestants are held in derision:

[29] *Ibid.*, Aug., 1928.   [30] Russell, *Studies in the Scriptures*, II, 276.
[31] Rutherford, *Jehovah's Witnesses: Why Persecuted?*
[32] Rutherford, *The Kingdom*, p. 13.

The Fundamentalists do not worship Jehovah as the only true God. They teach that Jesus and the "holy ghost" are equal to God. . . . They defame God's name by teaching the doctrine of eternal torture of men . . . and give their allegiance to the League of Nations.[33]

The clergy of both Roman Catholicism and Protestantism enjoy "indolent ease." [34] The Witnesses suggest that the clergy have devised religion as a source of cash income and of control over the people to whom they minister. Of all clergy, however, the Roman Catholic priest is most evil. Said a Witness: "I rejoice that the wicked Hierarchy is being stripped naked and exposed in all her shame so that all honest men may flee from her." [35] Moreover, Christians in general fail to demonstrate the love which their creeds proclaim. As one Witness said: "We find infidels who treat us better than these so-called Christian people whose God is Satan." [36]

The Roman Catholic Church, whether simply from experience or by official command, has of late shown a new attitude toward the movement. Up to 1941 the priests and laity viewed the Jehovah's Witnesses as enemies because of their attitude toward the Church. The Witnesses were vehement in retaliating; they called Catholics "evil," "wicked," "clergy-dominated," "stupid," and so on.[37] Many Catholics were unable to restrain themselves and fought back. They said that Witnesses had every right to worship as they pleased but not to attack the Roman Catholic Church. Assaults cannot be tolerated long by any religious group; they lead, if unanswered, to apostasy within the ranks. So the Catholics tried to discredit the Witnesses. The results were astonishingly discouraging. Persecution by the Catholics served to increase and strengthen the Witness membership. The futility of the policy of fight seemingly became quite apparent to the Catholics, and at the present moment the Roman Catholic Church is behaving as if the Jehovah's Witnesses does not exist. Its churchmen have refused to answer criticisms and in some cases have shown a courtesy and perseverance uncommon to their practice before 1941. The Witnesses have found this newer attitude baffling. For a time after they were being treated so "fairly," they tried to keep alive the cry of "the Roman Catholic evil," but their attempts, with few exceptions,

---

[33] Rutherford, *Who Is Your God?*, p. 61.
[34] Russell, *Studies in the Scriptures*, IV, 63.
[35] *Watch Tower*, June, 1936.   [36] *Ibid.*, May, 1930.
[37] See Rutherford, *Religion*, pp. 97, 301–302.

have met with complete failure, and the cause of hatred of the Roman Catholic Church is dying.

Not only is religion one of the three major evils of our time; commerce is another; politics is the third. The three are intimately interlinked, so that each does the bidding of the others, and the success of one is the success of all. According to Mr. Rutherford, corporations, "controlled by selfish men and aided by their political allies to give them a legal standing, carry out schemes of oppression." [38] Since most of the money of the world is lodged with the rich corporation owners, both religion and politics are the "stooges" of commerce.[39] Business is evil because it has enabled a few to amass the bulk of the wealth.

Society was divided by Mr. Russell into three "classes"—the upper, the middle, and the lower. Mr. Rutherford spoke more often of two— the wealthy and the poor. Wealth, arrogance, and pride are on one side, and widely prevailing poverty, ignorance, bigotry, and a keen sense of injustice are on the other.[40] Those who now are members of the wealthy class dominate and subjugate those who are poorer, but the division will not always remain the same:

The class coming into trouble has been used to luxury, obtained largely at the cost of others, among whom were some of the righteous, and out of them, because they resisted not, the very life had been crushed.[41]

The wealthy, according to the Witnesses, will be destroyed by Jehovah at the day of Judgment.[42]

The apparent similarity between what is known as the "Communist ideology" and some of the conceptions of the theology of the Jehovah's Witnesses has not yet dawned upon the Witnesses. As a people, the Russians were likened by Mr. Rutherford to the Amorites of ancient Hebrew times, evil, malicious, and "atheistic enemies of God." [43] Yet, the Witnesses use several concepts which may in essence be identified at least partially with the "Communist ideology." They believe that every society is divided according to "classes." These classes are in violent conflict for supremacy of power, and from the broad view, favor either the wealthy or the poor. The economic level of different segments of society seems to be the sole ground for defining a social "class," but in the re-

---

[38] Rutherford, *Hypocrisy*, p. 51.
[39] Rutherford, *The Crisis*, p. 6.
[40] Russell, *Studies in the Scriptures*, I, 325.
[41] *Ibid.*, p. 314.
[42] *Ibid.*, pp. 332–333.
[43] Rutherford, *The Kingdom*, p. 14.

ligious sphere the Witnesses use the word "class" to designate a group of like-minded persons, regardless of economic status.

The concept of "revolution" also plays a part in the ideology of the Witnesses. The founder of the movement spoke often of "the part which the coming social revolution MUST play in God's plan." [44] The final cataclysm is thus described by Mr. Russell: "Revolution, world-wide, will be the outcome, resulting in the final and complete destruction of the old order and the establishment of the new." [45] In what sense Jehovah could have a part in such a "revolution" Russell never fully explained, but from his descriptions of it (in their contexts) he seems, surprisingly, to imply that the revolution will be devised and executed by men without the aid of Jehovah. The imperfect conditions of present-day social organization cannot be ameliorated gradually by common assent because of the factor of power. Those who are in power will desire to continue their control: "Why cannot conditions be so altered as gradually to bring the equalization of wealth and comfort? Because the world is governed not by the royal law of love but by the law of depravity—selfishness." [46] The similarity to the "communistic" pattern is obvious.

Further, the struggle in which wealth will be wrested from those who have both wealth and power will be "amplitudinous"; in its final form it will entail world-wide war of the poor against the rich. Governments will presumably be on the side of the rich.

The gathering of the peoples of all nations in common interest in opposition to present governments is growing, and the result will be a uniting of the kingdoms for common safety, so that the trouble will be upon all kingdoms, and all will fall.[47]

In the final battle, the poor will triumph. The Witnesses depend upon that hope. "The fall of all kingdoms" is a part of their spiritual determinism, or "Destiny." Of this the Witnesses are sure: that the day of "world-wide blessings will not come as the majority have supposed, by peaceful evolution," [48] but by revolution. Thus, in spite of the hatred of the Witnesses for the Communists, they nevertheless employ certain conceptions of social change similar to those expressed by the Communist ideology.

The third significant hatred is that of politics. The Witnesses believe

---

[44] Russell, *Studies in the Scriptures*, II, 262.
[45] *Ibid.*, III, 59.   [46] *Ibid.*, IV, 305.   [47] *Ibid.*, I, 317.   [48] *Ibid.*, IV, Preface.

that the governments of all the nations, including the democratic, are ruled by Satan.[49] The fault with the social system does not lie upon the conscience of any one class; the prime difficulty has been the refusal by all to recognize and obey the will of Jehovah.[50] The entire social system is a product of "Christendom" whose demonic nature it reveals.[51] Although many nations claim to be guided by the Bible, nevertheless in actual practice they do not even refer to it:

Each session of the Congress of the United States is opened with a formal prayer uttered by some clergyman; but is the Bible advice ever sought or used as a guide for those law-makers? On the contrary, the laws of the earthly government are now invoked to prevent the people from hearing what is set forth in the Bible.[52]

The governments of the earth have failed because while rendering lip service to morality they have forgotten its true meaning.[53]

The presence of government, however, evil as it is, is better than no government at all:

Hence, while making no attempt to excuse our rebel race, we can sympathize with its main efforts to govern itself and to arrange for its own well-being. And something can be said of the success of the world in this direction; for, while recognizing the real character of these beastly governments, corrupt though they have been, they have been vastly superior to none—much better than lawlessness and anarchy.[54]

Moreover, it may even be "ordained" by God. This is not unlike the view expressed by Martin Luther. The Witness doctrine is as follows:

Evil as these Gentile governments have been, they were permitted or "ordained of God" for a wise purpose. Their imperfection and misrule form a part of the general lesson on the exceeding sinfulness of sin, and prove the inability of man to govern himself, even to his own satisfaction. God permits, in the main, men to carry out their own purposes as they may be able, overruling them only when they would interfere with his plans.[55]

Since national governments are wicked, the Witnesses generally do not hold office or vote. Their duty as they conceive it is to spread their message as universally as possible. They believe that they are God's am-

---

[49] Rutherford, *End of the Axis Powers.*
[50] Russell, *Studies in the Scriptures,* IV, 299.
[51] *Ibid.,* p. 96.　　[52] Rutherford, *Government,* p. 13.　　[53] *Ibid.,* p. 11.
[54] Russell, *Studies in the Scriptures,* I, 263.　　[55] *Ibid.,* p. 250.

bassadors from an alien land to the sinful men and women of the nations of the world. God's work is more important than man's. Moreover, the struggle does not depend upon men: "They [the saints] should remember that this is the Lord's battle, and that so far as politics or social questions are concerned, they have no real solution other than that predicted in the Word of God." [56] Mr. Russell warned all true believers that Jesus never tried to better the world through politics, and that his example was followed faithfully by the early apostles.[57] In their meetings the Witnesses have quoted Psalm 2: 1–6, 10–12, on the basis of which they picture themselves and Jehovah laughing at the vain rulers of the world. The tradition of not voting or holding office dates to the time of Russell, who advised his followers against such participation in politics.[58] The Witnesses sometimes refer with admiration to the refusal of the Reformed Presbyterians to vote on the grounds that the words "God" and "Christ" do not appear in the Constitution of the United States. The politically wise Witnesses also see that "he who votes at an election is morally bound to sustain the government he has participated in making —even to the giving of his life for its defence." [59]

Witnesses predict the downfall of every government. For a time this bold statement was readily accepted by many who wished to see a particular government, such as Hitler's or Stalin's, meet with disaster. These persons cheered the Witnesses on and openly said that perhaps they were correct in some of their other beliefs. The Witnesses and others recalled, however, that in his radio talk "Can the American Government Endure?" Mr. Rutherford predicted the fall even of the United States.[60] This news was less heartening. To Mr. Rutherford's mind, the United States could not survive the devastating effects of the economic depression of the thirties. The increase of unemployment and crime was interpreted as a sure sign of the coming doom of this country. Although the solution to the national problems could never be found in the theories of men, said Mr. Rutherford, men would still attempt to solve them themselves, without the aid of Jehovah. He predicted that President Hoover would group about himself certain "wise men" who would try to run the government "scientifically," but that even these would fail. Because of increasing social conflicts and blatant immoralities, it is Jehovah's will

---

[56] *Ibid.*, p. 342.   [57] *Ibid.*, p. 268.
[58] *Ibid.*, VI, 593.   [59] *Watch Tower*, Aug., 1893.
[60] "The American government has been weighed in the balance and found wanting. It cannot endure." Rutherford, *America's End*, p. 38.

that the government of the United States shall not endure. In answer to direct questions on this point Mr. Rutherford said: "From the Word of Jehovah I specifically answer the question, 'Can the American government endure?' And that answer is emphatically, 'No!' " [61] Startled Witnesses tried to accept the statement as "coming of the Lord" and then sought promptly to forget that it was ever made. Others received it as positive proof of the demonic character of the movement, and these withdrew.

According to Rutherford, it is folly to suppose that a form of government can last forever. God, being so great and powerful, cannot allow a human institution to usurp his place in the allegiance of the people. In this sense, Rutherford agrees with Tennyson that "our little systems" are "but broken lights of thee, and thou, O Lord, art more than they." But Rutherford goes further in that his views also imply that human institutions are not in any sense to be called "broken lights of thee." All human institutions are implacably evil, being ruled by Satan and not by Jehovah.

Carrying out his idea about the impermanency of the American form of government, Mr. Rutherford criticized the patriotism of those who think this country "eternal." Such superpatriotism tends to elevate the state to the supreme notch in the people's scale of values. When this is done, all "lesser" values lose their status, and even the family may be finally destroyed.[62]

Although the Witnesses theoretically have no "choice" in politics, in practice their views often become perceptible. For example, in the presidential election of 1940 many Witnesses obviously presented a Republican point of view. *Consolation* ran articles about the presidential election, including one letter from the former governor of Pennsylvania, Mr. Gifford Pinchot, who wrote opposing Mr. Roosevelt's election. The fact that Mr. Pinchot represented the "isolationist" point of view at that time likewise made him a valuable cohort.[63]

The Witnesses criticize "the good neighbor policy" of the United States, moreover, because to them it is based upon chicanery and selfishness. As one expressed it, "Too much love usually hides some evil." His thesis was that no country worthy of honor would go about the world voluntarily courting the respect and friendship of other nations. Deeply rooted in political pessimism, this Witness felt that the United States

[61] Rutherford, *Can the American Government Endure?* pp. 26–27.
[62] Russell, *Studies in the Scriptures*, IV, 490.   [63] *Consolation*, Oct., 1940.

"must be up to some trick." Some have told me that the United States desires the friendship of the other American countries only because it needs them in the war effort; others think that the United States merely wants raw materials and products and an outlet for its own commodities.

Yet, the Witnesses have great respect for the United States. Many of them evidence the marks of true patriotism, except in matters of flag saluting and the singing of the national anthem.

In recent years a number of cases involving flag saluting have been reported in the newspapers. The Witnesses say that they are willing to obey any government's laws which do not conflict with that which they conceive to be their essential duty to Jehovah. Saluting the flag, according to Mr. Rutherford, is very much like saying "Heil Hitler." It is an act which a true believer cannot conscientiously perform,[64] for, "according to authoritative definitions, the saluting of the flag is a religious ceremony which gives reverence and worship contrary to God's law." [65]

American citizens were for the most part divided in their opinion regarding the flag-saluting cases. Some of them, usually with super-patriotic motives, declared that any group, whether religious or not, which refuses to salute the flag of this country is subversive and detrimental to the cause of American democracy. They demanded the expulsion of the children from the public schools and the arrest of the parents. Other citizens, however, defended the right of the Witnesses to their stand. The sentiments of the Baltimore *Evening Sun* in the case of Carleton B. Nichols, Jr., a lad who refused to salute the flag and was summarily expelled from public school, were typical of those who condoned the refusal:

For our part, we glory in Carleton's spunk. Any statute requiring that the flag be saluted by school children is an insult to the Stars and Stripes, and ought to be resented by all patriots. Is our national ensign a swastika flag, to be respected only by forced salutes? Since when has the Star-Spangled Banner so lost the respect of the people over whom it waves that laws are necessary to make them pretend to honor it? What a disgraceful thing it is to assume that the flag would not be saluted if people were not afraid to refuse the tribute of respect! . . . It is supposed to float because its people have raised it of their own free will and uphold it out of preference—not because they fear it, but because they love it. If the time has come when they must be compelled to pay it a formal and forced tribute, the time has come to

---

[64] Rutherford, *Armageddon*, pp. 36–37.　　[65] Rutherford, *God and the State*, p. 17.

haul it down and hoist in its place some red or black banner of dictatorship of force and fear.[66]

Typical of the experiences of those Witnesses who refuse to salute the flag is the Gobitis case. The Gobitis family lived in a small Pennsylvania town where the children attended public school. The family were strict adherents of Witness teachings and for some years had indoctrinated their children with the necessity of refusing to salute the flag or to sing "America." The children believed that they had entered into a "covenant" with Jehovah which particularly forbade them to salute flags. Several years ago, however, the school board in the town, responding to a growing demand for "patriotism," ordered that all students should daily salute the flag. Because of their religious convictions, the Gobitis children asked to be excused and to remain silent during the patriotic exercises. For this they were promptly expelled.

When the case was reviewed in the United States District Court, the judge held that the children could not be compelled to salute the flag if in so doing they felt that they were violating their beliefs in God and in the sanctity of the Bible. In his decision the judge declared:

In these days, when religious intolerance is again rearing its ugly head in other parts of the world, it is of the utmost importance that the liberties guaranteed to our citizens by the fundamental law be preserved from all encroachment.

The school board, "although undoubtedly acting from patriotic motives, appears in this case to have become a means for the persecution of children for conscience's sake." Further the judge of the District Court said: "Our beloved flag, the emblem of religious liberty, apparently has been used as an instrument to impose a religious test as a condition of receiving the benefits of public education."

The Gobitis case unfortunately did not end at this point; after having passed the United States Circuit Court of Appeals, it was appealed finally, to the Supreme Court of the United States. The majority opinion of the Supreme Court overruled the decisions of the lower courts. It said that although individual citizens cannot be compelled to salute the flag, boards of education may make and enforce rules compelling the children under their jurisdiction to salute the flag as a condition of admission to the schools. The Supreme Court stated further that the

[66] Baltimore *Evening Sun*, Sept. 28, 1935.

whole question of flag saluting in the schools was largely a matter of educational strategy, and that the "court room is not the arena for debating issues of educational policy." If the Court were to decide the issue, then it held that it would become "the school board for the country." This responsibility it did not choose to assume.

The results of the Gobitis case were disastrous for the Witnesses. Shortly after the Supreme Court's decision was handed down, local school boards passed resolutions requiring the saluting of the flag as a condition for receiving public education. The Witnesses experienced in many parts of the country, mainly in small towns and rural areas, a form of persecution which only made most of them even more determined never to coöperate with government in any matter. In a conflict between loyalty to the state and loyalty to God, they chose God.

Recently the attitude of some school boards has changed. Today those Witnesses who will not salute the flag are oftentimes ignored. One of the Witnesses in a small town said that his daughter had refused to salute the flag in the classroom where the teacher was obviously able to notice it. When the teacher failed to keep the child after class or demand why she had not participated in the patriotic exercises, the child went to the teacher and said: "Didn't you see that I didn't salute the flag?" The teacher replied that she had noticed. Then the child asked: "Ain't you gonna do anything about it?" When the teacher said that she was not, the child walked away bewildered. While on the surface this seems a more desirable way to treat the problem, it is believed by some not to solve it. They hold that the school should seek to make the meaning of government and of conflicting loyalties clear through discussion, and should never allow the matter of flag saluting to break down the confidence of the children in their teachers and in their schools.

The Witnesses are mainly concerned with the coming age, however, and feel that all of the hustle and bustle of men here and now will pass, when Jehovah ends the present age and introduces believers into the heavenly delight. Men now are missing the whole point of life. The situation as seen by the Witnesses is well described by the words of Machiavelli: "Men often act like certain small birds of prey, who, prompted by their nature, pursue their victims so eagerly that they do not see the larger bird above them, ready to pounce down upon and kill them." [67]

The Witnesses have always felt that a positive sign of the coming

[67] *Discourses*, Chap. XL.

end of the age was the banning of their movement by all nations. The crushing of the Jehovah's Witnesses in Germany with the rise to power of Adolf Hitler had an electrifying effect upon the morale of the Witnesses in this country. Instead of feeling discouraged they rejoiced and looked forward with eager anticipation to similar actions in other countries. When Australia and Canada barred the organization, the Witnesses in this country took further hope that the age was fast closing. Now they are almost jubilantly anticipating the closing of the work of the movement by the government of the United States. In such an eventuality the Witnesses feel that the kingdom would be very close at hand. In the countries in which they have been banned they have not tried to do more than assert constitutionally conceived rights of free speech and free press. They do not resort to force against governments which fail to recognize these as inalienable rights of all citizens, for the movement has from the beginning been unanimous upon that point: "We must not present the truth through lawless means." [68] Similarly Mr. Rutherford often stated that his followers should not use force against the existing governments. The Witness must refuse to obey any national law which to him is contrary to the law of God, but even in such a situation the Witness must not seek to remedy the national laws. He must accept his fate with a stolid reliance upon God: "Every nation has laws, and every citizen of such nation must obey those laws unless the law is in direct violation or contravention of God's law." [69]

The law of God forbids Witnesses to engage in war. The view has commonly been taken that they are pacifists. Such they are not, for they feel that they must often employ physical force to resist persecution, and they also believe that Jehovah has engaged in and encouraged wars between peoples. The Witnesses will not engage in the present war because they think that Jehovah is not concerned with it; otherwise they would be quite willing to fight. Most of them believe that Satan is "running the whole show" and therefore they will have nothing to do with it. This is similar to their attitude toward the first World War. Then Witnesses were interned by both sides, because the Society boldly stated that the war was being fought by equally selfish interests and without the sanction of God. Their own fight, they declared, was not fought with "carnal weapons"; [70] it was a battle of cosmic proportions with the adversary of every man, Satan. The passages of the Old Testament which involve

[68] *Watch Tower*, Aug., 1889.   [69] Rutherford, *Supremacy*, p. 51.
[70] Russell, *Studies in the Scriptures*, IV, 549.

war have been pointed out to the Witnesses as constituting a special problem for anyone who presumes that God does not take part in wars. The Witnesses think that Jehovah was connected with the battles recorded in the Old Testament, otherwise he would not have permitted accounts of them to be inserted in the Bible. Mr. Rutherford said that such wars were justified because they involved "the execution of his (God's) judgment against workers of wickedness." [71] Seemingly, God no longer executes his judgment through the wars of men.

Witnesses have sought exemption from the Selective Service Act on the grounds that they are duly appointed ministers.[72] Local draft boards have decided variously on this point. Some have accepted the statement of status as ministers of religion, while others have decided that the Witnesses are not really ministers because they are not formally licensed by any religious group. Some draft boards have refused to recognize as a valid license the card which the Witnesses carry stating that they are officially connected with the Watch Tower Bible and Tract Society. *The Conscientious Objector*,[73] for example, regularly lists many Witnesses who have been interned on these grounds.

In most cases, the Witnesses cannot be exempted on the basis of conscientious objection to war. Some of them may be opposed to the present conflict but not to war as such, and this attitude does not constitute sufficient reason for exemption. The genuine conscientious objectors among the Jehovah's Witneses are usually interned in camps belonging to pacifist organizations. *Fellowship*, the official organ of the Fellowship of Reconciliation, has occasionally described the position of these interned Witnesses. Presumably they follow fairly well the life which is laid down for them in the camps. There are a number of cases, however, of Witnesses who have refused to register for the draft, or to appear before their local boards for examination, or to report when sentenced to work camps. Like the Pennsylvania Moravians, some Witnesses are convinced that to allow the government to regulate any area of an individual's life is tantamount to the surrender of personal liberty and responsibility to God.

Through Mr. Covington, formerly the chief legal representative, the Society has declared its views to the Department of Justice. In his

---

[71] Rutherford, *Justifying War*, p. 54.   [72] *Consolation*, Oct., 1940.

[73] A leading pacifist organ, published monthly by the Conscientious Objectors' Press, New York.

letter to the Department, Covington stated that every Witness should be "responsible for his own acts and decisions," but that the Society wished to be regarded as neutral toward all combatant nations.

The Witnesses hold that all of the nations involved are equally guilty of war preparations and incidents and that the task of every believer is to remain aloof from the struggle and to preach the coming destruction, of which the present war is only the beginning.

Just before his death, Mr. Rutherford published a small pamphlet entitled *End of the Axis Powers: Comfort All That Mourn.* The thesis of this pamphlet tends to establish a newer line of opinion among the Witnesses. To what extent it will be accepted remains to be seen. Mr. Rutherford proclaimed to the Witnesses that all of the nations of the world are condemned by Jehovah. Although this belief had been stated before, nevertheless, to it had now been attached the conception that both the Axis powers and the United Nations will definitely be destroyed. Neither side had recognized the theocracy, which is sufficient reason for Jehovah to condemn any or all nations.

The facts are indisputable, and therefore admitted, that the Nazis, Fascists, and the mightiest religious organization on earth, acting together and designated as "the Axis powers," now rule from Norway to Egypt and within that realm the people mourn. That ruling power is opposed to the Kingdom of God under Christ and violently opposes everyone who advocates THE THEOCRACY.[74]

The United Nations are characterized in the following manner:

Opposing the Nazi, powerful religious combine is another mighty world power, carried on by the political and commercial strong men of these nations, and ably supported by the religious leaders. That world power is generally known as the advocate of Democracy, and during the World War from 1914 to 1918 adopted and used the slogan: "This war will make the world safe for democracy." That ruling power does not advocate the kingdom and hence is against THE THEOCRACY.[75]

I have found that most Witnesses are ready to accept the defeat of the Axis countries but that few of them really desire the annihilation of the United Nations. The exact details of the end of both of these opposing powers could not be foreseen by Mr. Rutherford, but he did assure his readers that when the time came they would be able to read

[74] Rutherford, *End of the Axis Powers*, p. 10. [75] *Ibid.*

all about it in *The Watch Tower*. He also gave this assurance; when the end of the present war comes, then "God's kingdom of righteousness shall rule the people right here in earth, and they shall rejoice."

The message of Mr. Rutherford, like a voice from the grave, haunts the Witnesses. They do not know whether they are quite willing to believe and trust this doctrine of "the last days" to the point that they would be willing to advocate openly the destruction of the United Nations. But their hope is steadfast that in the newly established kingdom the Witnesses, who are the righteous people, will find the fulfillment of their long-anticipated desire.

Bibliography

PRIMARY SOURCES

The Watch Tower Bible and Tract Society, Brooklyn, N.Y., publishes the literature of the Jehovah's Witnesses, including two official magazines:

The Watch Tower Announcing Jehovah's Kingdom. This was founded in July, 1879, as a monthly (published biweekly from 1893) called *Zion's Watch Tower and Herald of Christ's Presence,* and was under the editorship of Charles T. Russell until 1916. From 1908 to 1938 it was called *The Watch Tower and Herald of Christ's Presence;* in January and February, 1939, it was known as *The Watch Tower and Herald of Christ's Kingdom,* and thereafter by its present name.

Consolation was founded in October, 1919, as *The Golden Age* and received its present name in October, 1937.

CHARLES TAZE RUSSELL

Food for Thinking Christians. Allegheny, Pa., n.d. Probably published c. 1880.

Millennial Dawn. *See* Studies in the Scriptures.

Pastor Russell's Sermons: a Choice Collection of His Most Important Discourses on all Phases of Christian Doctrine and Practice. Brooklyn, N.Y. Published posthumously.

Photo-Drama of Creation, and Religious Speeches. Brooklyn, N.Y., 1917.

Studies in the Scriptures: a Helping Hand for Bible Students. 7 vols. Allegheny, Pa. 1897–1902. Also called Millennial Dawn: the Divine Plan of the Ages, and the Corroborative Testimony of the Great Pyramid in Egypt, God's Stone Witness and Prophet.

Thy Word Is Truth: an Answer to Robert Ingersoll's Charges against Christianity. Allegheny, Pa., n.d. Announced as No. 15 of "Old Theology Tracts for the Promotion of Christian Knowledge."

JOSEPH FRANKLIN RUTHERFORD

Since Mr. Rutherford wrote many dozens of books and several hundred pamphlets, a listing of them all would exceed the interests of this bibliography. Therefore, a careful selection is here offered. All of the following titles were published by the Watch Tower Bible and Tract Society, Brooklyn, N.Y.

America's End. 1934.

Angels. 1934.

Armageddon. 1937.

Beyond the Grave. 1934.

Can the American Government Endure? 1933.

Can the Living Talk with the Dead? 1920.

The Cause of Death. 1932.

Children. 1941.

Creation. 1927.

The Crisis. 1933.

Deliverance. 1926.

The End of the Axis Powers. 1941.

Enemies. 1937.

Escape to the Kingdom. 1933.

Face the Facts. 1938.

Fascism or Freedom? 1939.

God and the State. 1941.

Government. 1935.

Government and Peace. 1939.

A Great Battle in the Ecclesiastical Heavens. 1915.

The Harp of God. 1921.

Health and Life. 1932.

The Hereafter. 1932.

Hypocrisy. 1932.

Intolerance. 1933.

Jehovah. 1934.

Jehovah's Organization. 1932.

Jehovah's Witnesses: Why Persecuted? 1933.

Jews. 1934.

Judge Rutherford Uncovers the Fifth Column. 1940.

Justifying War. 1934.

The Kingdom. 1931.

The Last Days. 1928.

Liberty. 1932.

Life. 1929.

Light. 2 vols., 1930.

Loyalty. 1935.

Marriage. 1936.

Millions Now Living Will Never Die. 1920. (Numerous reissues.)

Preparation. 1933.

Preservation. 1932.

Prophets Foretell Redemption. 1932.

Refugees. 1940.

Religion. 1940.

Religions. 1934.

Religious Intolerance: Why? 1933.

Restoration. 1927.

Riches. 1936.

Safety, Comfort. 1937.

Salvation. 1939.

Supremacy. 1939.

The Theocracy. 1941.

Universal War Near. 1935.

Vindication. 3 vols., 1931–32.

Warning. 1938.

What Is Truth? 1932.

Who Is Your God? 1934.

Who Shall Rule the World? 1935.

Why Serve Jehovah? 1936.

World Recovery. 1934.

OTHER PRIMARY SOURCES

It is unlikely that these were written by either Mr. Russell or Mr. Rutherford, but they comprise official literature of the Watch Tower Bible and Tract Society, Brooklyn, N.Y.

Yearbook. Published annually since 1933.

Model Study, Nos. 1 to 3. 1937–41.

Liberty to Preach. n.d. Written by Mr. Olin Moyle.

Jehovah's Servants Defended. 1941. Probably written by Mr. Covington.

SECONDARY SOURCES

Aldred, Guy Alfred. Armageddon, Incorporated. Glasgow, Scotland, 1941. 35 pp.

American Civil Liberties Union. The Persecution of the Jehovah's Witnesses: the Record of Violence against a Religious Organization Unparalleled in America since the Attacks on the Mormons. New York, 1941.

———— Jehovah's Witnesses and the War. New York, 1943. 36 pp.

Baalen, Jan K. van. Our Birthright and the Mess of Meat: Isms of Today Analyzed and Compared with the Heidelberg Catechism. Grand Rapids, Mich., 1919. One chapter is devoted to the Jehovah's Witnesses.

Barbour, Nelson, H. Through Worlds, and the Harvest of This World. . . . Rochester, N.Y., 1877. 194 pp.

Biederwolf, W. E. Russellism Unveiled. Grand Rapids, Mich., n.d. 35 pp.

Braeunlich, Paul. Die Ernsten Bibelforscher als Opfer bolschewistischer Religionsspötter. Leipzig, 1926. 40 pp.

Brooks, Keith. Prophetic Program of Judge Rutherford. Los Angeles, Calif., n.d. 12 pp.

Burridge, J. H. Pastor Russell's Date System and Teaching on the Person of Christ. New York, n.d. 30 pp.

———— Pastor Russell's Position and Credentials and His Methods of Interpretation. New York, n.d. 32 pp.

———— Pastor Russell's Teaching on the Coming of Christ. New York, n.d. 31 pp.

Cook, Charles. More Data on Pastor Russell. New York, n.d. 30 pp.

———— All about One Russell. Philadelphia, n.d. 24 pp.

Cooper, G. H. Millennial Dawnism or Satan in Disguise. Swengel, Pa., n.d. 10 pp.

Czatt, Milton Stacey. The International Bible Students: Jehovah's Witnesses. (Yale Studies in Religion, No. 4.) Scottsdale, Pa., 1933. 43 pp.

Fardon, A. H., and H. J. McFarland. Jehovah's Witnesses: Who Are They; What Do They Teach? Chicago, 1941. 21 pp.

Ferguson, Charles W. The Confusion of Tongues. New York, 1928. 464 pp. One chapter on the Jehovah's Witnesses.

Forrest, James Edward. Errors of Russellism: a Brief Examination of the Teachings of Pastor Russell as Set Forth in His "Studies of the Scriptures." Anderson, Ind., 1915. 277 pp.

Freyenwald, Jonah von. Die Zeugen Jehovas: Pioniere für ein Judisches Weltreich die politischen Ziele der internationalen Vereinigung Ernster Bibelforscher. Berlin, 1936. 103 pp.

Gray, James. The Errors of Millennial Dawnism. Chicago, 1920. 24 pp.

—— Satan and the Saint: the Present Darkness and the Coming Light. Chicago, 1909. 124 pp. One chapter on the Jehovah's Witnesses.

Haldeman, Isaac Massey. Millennial Dawnism: the Blasphemous Religion Which Teaches the Annihilation of Jesus Christ. New York, 1910. 80 pp.

—— Two Men and Russellism. New York, 1915. 63 pp.

Hewitt, Paul Edward. Russellism Exposed. Grand Rapids, Mich., 1941. 6 pp.

High, Stanley. "Armageddon, Inc." *Saturday Evening Post*, Sept., 14, 1940.

Irvine, W. C. Heresies Exposed: an Exposure of Some of the Prevailing Heresies of the Day. 11th ed. New York, 1940. 225 pp. One chapter on the Jehovah's Witnesses.

Johnson, Thomas Cary. Some Modernisms. Richmond, Va., 1919. 192 pp. One chapter on the Jehovah's Witnesses.

Lienhardt, Hans. Ein Riesenverbrechen am deutschen Volke und die Ernsten Bibelforscher. 2d ed. 1921. 46 pp.

Maynard, John Albert. Russellism. London, 1936. 31 pp.

Meyenberg, Albert. Ueber die sogenannten Ernsten Bibelforscher: Geschichte, Lehre und Kritik. Luzern, 1924. 19 pp.

Moorhead, W. G. Remarks on Millennial Dawn. New York, 1891. 4 pp.

Nyman, Aaron. Astounding Errors: the Prophetic Message of the Seventh-day Adventists and the Chronology of Pastor C. T. Russell in the Light of History and Bible Knowledge. Chicago, 1914. 419 pp.

"Peddlers of Paradise." *The American Magazine*, Nov., 1940.

Pollock, A. J. Examination of Judge Rutherford's Books. New York, n.d. 15 pp.

—— Millennial Dawnism: Briefly Tested by the Scripture. London, 1917. 23 pp.

—— How Russell Died. New York, n.d.

Putnam, C. E. Jehovah's Witnesses: Russellism; Rutherfordism—Are They God's Prophets? Randleman, N.C., n.d. 6 pp.

Reid, R. J. How Russellism Subverts the Faith. New York, n.d. 69 pp.

Ross, J. J. Some Facts and More Facts about the Self-styled Pastor Charles T. Russell of Millennial Dawn Fame. Philadelphia, n.d. 48 pp.

Saleeby, Abdallah Assed. Truth Triumphant: or, Falsehood Stripped of Its Mask. Norfolk, Va., 1919. 145 pp.

Shadduck, B. H. The Seven Thunders of Millennial Dawn. Philadelphia, 1934. 32 pp. 1st ed. 1928.

Shields, T. T. Russellism, Rutherfordism: the Teachings of the International Bible Students Alias Jehovah's Witnesses in the Light of Holy Scriptures. Grand Rapids, Mich., 1934. 106 pp.

Smith, R. T.   Jehovah's Witnesses: Millennial Dawnism or Russellism and Rutherfordism—What Do They Teach? Philadelphia, n.d. 8 pp.

Stewart, E. D. "Life of Pastor Russell." *Overland Monthly*, LXXIX (San Francisco, 1917), 126–132.

Stroup, Herbert.   "The Attitude of the Jehovah's Witnesses toward the Roman Catholic Church." *Religion in the Making*, II, No. 2 (Jan., 1942), 148–163.

———— "Class Theories of the Jehovah's Witnesses." *Social Science*, XIX, No. 2 (April, 1944).

Walker, Charles.   "Fifth Column Jitters." *McCall's Magazine*, November, 1940.

Woodworth, William Norman.   God and Reason by Frank Fact Finder (pseud.). Brooklyn, N.Y., 1934. 124 pp.

Wyrick, Herbert.   Seven Religious Isms. Grand Rapids, Mich., n.d. 99 pp. One chapter on the Jehovah's Witnesses.

Zurcher, Franz.   Kreuzzug gegen das Christentum. Zurich, 1938. 214 pp.

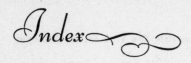

Index